Finding Voice

Finding Voice

How Theological Field Education
Shapes Pastoral Identity

WILLIAM B. KINCAID

WIPF & STOCK · Eugene, Oregon

FINDING VOICE
How Theological Field Education Shapes Pastoral Identity

Wipf & Stock
An Imprint of Wipf and Stock Publishers
199 W. 8th Ave., Suite 3
Eugene, OR 97401
www.wipfandstock.com

ISBN 13: 978-1-61097-694-7

Manufactured in the U.S.A.

To Rhonda, Andrew, and Maggie

The voices I cherish most

Contents

Acknowledgments

I AM THANKFUL TO be in ministry with the Christian Theological Seminary community and am especially grateful to the trustees, administration, and faculty at CTS for the research leave that afforded me time to complete this work.

A number of people read and commented on small parts of this book at various stages of its development. I appreciate their interest, encouragement, and feedback. I especially want to thank Linda McCrae, Judy Fackenthal, and Dale Matherly for taking time from their pastoral work to read most of this book and make extensive and helpful comments.

I also want to thank Christian Amondson at Wipf and Stock for his support of this project and Mike van Mantgem whose attentive editing and helpful suggestions significantly improved portions of this book.

Introduction

When you truly possess all you have been and done,
you are fierce with reality.[1]

—FLORIDA SCOTT MAXWELL

IMAGINE THAT YOU ARE the student pastor at Rosy Ridge Church. In the short time of six weeks you have left the suburbs of a major city, enrolled in seminary, and moved to a village that is twenty-five miles away from the nearest Walmart Supercenter. The parsonage phone rings at 2 a.m. Your sleep-dazed hello is interrupted with a frightened voice. "Pastor, it's our two-year old, Kevin. He had a seizure. We're at University Hospital and he's had two more seizures in the last hour. The doctors don't know what the problem is. They may have to put him on a ventilator. Can you come?"

"Sure," you say, "I'm on my way." You dress, try to put a face with the name you just heard on the phone, walk through the still country night to your car, and nervously rattle the key into the ignition. The small towns along Highway 11 feature more activity the closer you get to the city. Your thoughts bounce between "What will I say to the family?" to "Where will I park?"

The large parking structure is mostly empty. You quickly pull between two yellow stripes and park the car. You climb three flights of a concrete stairwell, hurry across a pedway into the hospital, and begin looking for the pediatrics unit. You discover that it's on the fifth floor. You weave through a maze of waiting rooms and vacated registration desks, and down the hall to an elevator. Once on the fifth floor you recognize

---

1. Maxwell, *Measure*, 42.

Kevin's parents in the hallway. They are talking to a group of physicians. The doctors slip into a consulting room as you approach.

"Oh, thank God, you are here." They say. Both parents hug you, dropping tears on your jacket. "Kevin isn't breathing on his own. Why would something like this happen? They just put him on a ventilator and said the next twenty-four hours are critical. We want you to baptize him, you know, just in case."

What now? Just six weeks ago you were a computer programmer, or a chemist, or a retail salesperson, or a stay-at-home parent. You were something other than the student pastor at Rosy Ridge Church. Now, you are standing outside a pediatric intensive care unit at 3 a.m. beside two parents who are facing the greatest fear they can imagine. They have turned to you for answers and action. In that moment, you are not speaking or acting only for yourself, but as the pastor of Rosy Ridge Church. What do you say? And what do you do?

Finding Voice will guide seminarians to discover what is essential in the development of a clear and vigorous pastoral identity by probing and reflecting on the most germane and significant aspects of their supervised ministry, contextual education and field education experiences. This book is a textbook for learning ministry that uses the contextual, supervised component of theological education as its starting point.

Ministry is comprised of conversations and events like this. These crisis events cause us to consider penetrating and troubling questions. Who am I as a minister in a moment like that? How does my pastoral identity inform my response? How does the Christian story inform my response? What personal issues and needs do I bring to such an encounter? To what extent do local cultural norms and congregational practices determine what I say and do?

Your field education experiences intentionally expose you to moments like these and press you to reflect on them through pastoral and theological lenses. Through the process of engaging a particular cultural context and identifying its theological views and commitments, performing pastoral roles, thinking about who you are as a person and who you are becoming as a minister, and participating in family and congregational systems, you will begin to understand and claim your pastoral identity. This is to say, your field education helps you to find your voice as a minister.[2]

2. Seminaries and divinity schools use a variety of terms to refer to the component of

While rooted in common language and practices, the pastoral voice varies from person to person. What is authentic for one individual may feel disingenuous to another. Like every person who has ever walked through the doors of a seminary or divinity school, you are, in the words of the psalmist, "fearfully and wonderfully made."[3] You bring to your field education study a wide variety of experiences and perspectives, celebrations and sorrows. You probably also carry within you more than a few questions about how this journey will unfold and what particular direction your vocational path will take. As with other parts of the theological curriculum, you may discover your field education experiences generate far more questions than answers. You are, after all, learning about life in a place that may be quite different from which you are accustomed. Congregational dynamics and cultural influences will likely swirl around you. You will spend time learning the names of people in your congregation and, at the same time, try to figure out who you are as a minister. You may learn things about your faith tradition that you never knew, and perhaps things you did not really want to know.

The practice of ministry calls for reflection, which in turn leads to reappraisal. As a result, when a minister does something for the second or third or fourth time, whether it be preaching a sermon or facilitating a meeting or participating in a community project, he or she can approach it with the benefit of experience, reflection, and reappraisal.

My colleague Dan Moseley, an avid jazz fan, says that learning ministry is like learning to play a musical instrument. On Dan's desk is a quote from Charlie Parker: "Music is your own experience. It is your thoughts, your wisdom. If you don't live it, it won't come out of your horn."[4] As Moseley writes, "It is your music that you know—from inside your soul. It isn't just music that you construct in your head or music you inherited

---

theological studies wherein student learning grows out of their service in a congregation or community ministry. These terms include "field education," "supervised ministry," and "contextual education." Requirements, emphases, and expectations vary from school to school. In some cases, the field education requirement can be fulfilled by completing two semester-long internships. In other programs, a full two or even three years are required. While this book focuses on ministry in a congregational setting, your field education may include ministry in an institutional or agency setting as well. Your church tradition will influence and perhaps even dictate where you serve, and for how long.

3. Ps 139:14.

4. Moseley, "Playing Jazz."

from others, but it is music that comes from the inside of the body and soul as well as the head and heart."[5]

If you are enrolled in a field education program, you should learn practical matters such as the details of worship services, the priorities of congregational administration, and the structures of organizational governance. But, in truth, you are immersed in ministry sites for a more essential reason, and that is to explore and claim your own pastoral identity. By engaging the various facets of a ministry placement, field education provides you with a process that allows you to discover the pastoral music that lives in your body and soul. Craig Dykstra captures this idea of voice when he writes:

> It is a beautiful thing to see a good pastor at work. Somehow, pastors who really get what the Christian ministry is all about and do it well are able to enter many diverse situations, whether joyous or full of misery and conflict, and see what is going on there through the eyes of faith. This way of seeing and interpreting shapes what the pastor thinks and does and how he or she responds to people in gestures, words, and actions. It functions as a kind of internal gyroscope, guiding pastors in and through every crevice of pastoral life and work.[6]

Navigating these situations is not always easy. For example, in some cases we see a total abandonment of pastoral voice when churches and ministers choose not to address issues of war, discrimination, and poverty. In other cases, we hear a shrill, overreaching voice from churches and ministers that oversimplifies situations, condemns those who think or act differently, and remains unaware of its own prejudices and vulnerabilities. As you give yourself over to this journey, your pastoral voice will calibrate itself while leading and responding to various people and situations. Your pastoral voice ought not be used for your own political safety or professional advancement. Rather, your voice should be used to give strong theological and pastoral leadership when opportunities and challenges occur in the church and community.

You will make some missteps. In fact, some of your most important learning may come from experimentation and mistakes. Supervised ministry provides you with an environment to do just that. But you do not

---

5. Ibid.

6. Dykstra, "Pastoral and Ecclesial Imagination," 41.

need to confine experimentation in ministry to a seminary internship. The pastoral life is one of continuous learning. Unfortunately, too many pastors develop such a cautious and timid voice that their greatest opportunities for learning—not to mention their most exciting moments in ministry—never occur.

The difference between confidence and timidity in ministry is the quality of pastoral voice. An otherwise cautious minister who has found a strong pastoral voice can speak powerfully and convincingly from his or her own experience and from the riches of Scripture and Christian tradition. As a result, these ministers lovingly and purposefully shape communities of faith to be hospitable and prophetic places, take courageous stands for fairness in the community, critique the enticing fads and seductive trends that do not represent the gospel, and serve with an eye toward God's presence and purposes in the world. Those who find voice live "obediently in the center of a call,"[7] and those who avoid voice bide their time until, hopefully, they feel a claim on their lives persuasive enough to engage what really stirs and energizes them. Without voice, pastors abdicate their pastoral responsibilities, manipulate people and situations in coercive ways, and function as technicians who fill their days with a series of seemingly unrelated and unimportant tasks.

Consider how the following six issues create the clarifying environment that a minster needs to find voice.

First, when you begin your work it will be with a specific congregation in a particular place at a given time. This congregation will present you with its own set of practices, gifts, opportunities, wounds, and challenges. All the vagaries of "church" will disappear as you immerse yourself in the particularities of this one congregation. As a result, your ministry will take shape not in the safety of the theoretical, though those discussions are helpful, but in the realities of that intersection where the worlds of hope and despair collide. You will encounter creativity and caution, promise and pessimism in all its individual and shared dimensions.

Second, while people think of field education as a practical component of theological education, your field education experience will offer you constant ways of interacting with and interpreting the greater story of the Christian faith. For example, many of Christianity's conflicts have played out through the church's worship. Some of those conflicts will be

7. MacDonald, "God's Callling Plan," 35–42.

apparent in the worship setting and practice at your ministry site. You also will connect to the greater story of faith by noting your congregation's system of governance, its stances on social issues, and in the way your congregation relates to its own denomination, as well as to other Christian and non-Christian traditions. Again, ministry in the abstract might allow you to avoid such distinctions, but you will not be ordained to serve in the realm of the theoretical. Your faith to this point will have been shaped by engagement with the particulars of the Christian story, for good or ill, even if you do not recognize it at the time. You may not agree with everything that your tradition believes, but at the very least you will be ordained within the parameters of a specific church. Finding your pastoral voice requires that you wrestle with your tradition in order to interpret your faith in a lively and credible manner.

Third, consider how performing various pastoral roles and working in different areas of congregational life will allow you to test your calling against what you have perceived your calling to be thus far, and what to that point has held the most interest for you in ministry. Some who initially saw themselves as chaplains prior to field education may be drawn to parish life and leadership. Others who once craved the chance to work on social justice issues in the wider community may discover that their passion lies more with preaching and leading worship. These paths, of course, are not mutually exclusive, but are offered as examples of ways that people might experience their vocational journey. Hopefully, those who preach do so always with an eye and heart for social justice and those who administer social programs value the care of souls. Voice arises from understanding your gifts and passions and then finding your place on a vocational path that allows you to give full expression to those gifts and passions.

Fourth, field education provides occasions for you to understand yourself more fully as a person in ministry. The difference between how extroverts and introverts approach ministry may not come into clear focus until you have spent the better part of the day either preparing for a Bible study or traveling with the church's seniors group. Hopefully, you will have some notion of what emotional issues hook you prior to serving a congregation. But encountering someone in the church who treats you like a domineering parent, or distrustful partner, or a watchful elementary school principal can trigger responses and actions from you that can compromise your ministry, damage your relationships with the congregation, and reveal brokenness that calls for therapeutic attention. From the time we are very young we try out other people's voices in an attempt to better understand who we are and are not. Field education is a clarifying experience that enables you to find and then claim your own pastoral voice.

Fifth, plans and strategies in ministry can remain exceptionally clear-cut until we attempt to implement them in the sea of ambiguity that characterizes most congregations. People show up at meetings with various joys, needs, histories, and agendas, many of which they are not even aware of having. You, of course, will often show up to these meetings equally loaded with ambiguity, but hopefully you will be more aware of the burdens you carry. Not until you try to effect change within a system that is determined to stay just the way it is can you appreciate the grace and persistence required of you to effectively function in your pastoral role. Pastors very often develop strong and fairly healthy relationships with parishioners on a one-on-one basis. Even so, these same pastors can naively get caught in the crosshairs of congregational conflict because they fail to understand and pay attention to the emotional dimension of a church system. So, for example, in addition to knowing that a particular church member is anxious about her upcoming surgery, her pastor also must recognize where the anxiety in the church family currently is manifesting itself because of this and other events in the congregation, and what shifts are occurring within the system to accommodate or resist that anxiety. Pastoral voice involves both an understanding of congregational dynamics and a healthy, agile self-differentiation from the congregation itself. To effect change in the congregation requires that you, as pastor, have a certain ability to recalibrate your agenda such that you can still move the congregation forward without overwhelming the system.

And sixth, field education provides you with real-time opportunities to understand how all of these dynamics function in relation to one another.

Just as these issues inform and interpret one another in our personal and pastoral lives, so the chapters in this book inform and interpret one another. We cannot artificially divide ministry in ways that allow us to keep key issues at arm's length from each other. Each one of these issues is always at play in congregational life and leadership. By the same token, we cannot separate the faith story from the contextual trends any more than we stop our own personal journeys from influencing our practice of ministry or of shaping our participation in a congregational system. Your ministry will not unfold in a tidy sequence. Rather, you will experience many of the issues explored in the pages of this book all at once. What's more, these issues often will surface in tension with one another.

Pastoral voice is diminished when any of the aforementioned six issues are missing. For example, a pastor may start pulling practical plans and programs out of her ministerial bag of tricks soon upon arrival without first pausing long enough to become acquainted with the twists and turns of the congregation's story and the complexities of its context. A few painful weeks or months later she finally realizes that she has offered a set of answers to questions that nobody was asking. In this case, some of the practical skills that are so essential to pastoral voice are present, but because ministry is contextual these skills become a source of conflict. Skills alone do not add up to pastoral voice.

Or consider the pastor who sees ministry primarily in terms of pastoral care to individuals. He may be known throughout the community for spending incredible blocks of time with those who are hospitalized, confined to their homes, or enduring some personal or family crisis. Everyone celebrates and appreciates his presence and compassion in those troubling times, but within the congregation there is a growing sense of his ineffectiveness in leading the congregation's ministry and mission. He appears to be clueless about how to effect change and deal with sabotage within the congregational system. As a result, his unawareness of the dynamics going on all around him mutes his pastoral voice, and so his ministry gets reduced to that of a congregational chaplain.

Or think about the self-differentiated pastor with a remarkable grasp of group process who only draws from the world of psychology and therapy and does not bring the life-giving resources of the Christian story into the conversation. Healing, thanks be to God, comes from numerous professional arenas and disciplines, and every pastor should engage in the broadest conversations possible. But pastoral voice consistently and intentionally looks to Scripture, theology, and the traditions of the church for its grounding.

Or what about those pastors who cannot connect these areas and may even find that such integration cramps their style? They may understand themselves and their context, live out their roles well in the midst of many claims on their time and energy, and even refer ably to the Christian story, but they always seem to hold it all in tidy compartments that have nothing to say to each other, or to the pastors themselves, or to the pressing issues of the day that long for some interpretation and good news. It is as if these pastors maintain a professional distance from the claims and complexities of ministry, which then insures that none of this seeps too deeply into their own bones. Their work lacks soul.

As novelist Laraine Herring says, deep, authentic writing occurs when we merge with what we are writing. She describes writing as "dissolving our egos so that the real work can emerge through us, without our conditions for success attached to it."[8] So it is with ministry. Pastoral voice cannot develop when we keep the concerns of ministry at arm's length. It surfaces and grows when we bring all of who we are—our gifts, hope, uncertainty, and fragility—to our work. And so, in addition to completing courses in Bible, history, theology, ethics, and practical parish ministry, the pressing question around finding your voice as a minister is this: Where are you in this process? Are you

- Sufficiently present and committed to your field education ministry site or already considering the next stop in your career?

- Understanding this ministry internship to be a season of intense learning or looking for ways to punch your degree worksheet?

- Discerning the vocational path that awakens and energizes you or still living under somebody else's map for your life?

- Informing your ministry with the depth and breadth of a life-giving faith or searching far and wide for a slogan or gimmick to temporarily pacify a few restless congregants?

- Tending to the personal issues with an eye for sustaining effective ministry with integrity or avoiding the very things that trip you up, bring down your ministry, and set back the church?

- Working calmly and courageously with the messiness of ministry or being swept away by personal disillusionment and congregational anxiety?

- Bringing all of this together in a way that obviously matters to you and speaks to the ultimate concerns of individual and communal life or keeping all of this at bay for selective use that will not involve many personal or professional risks?

8. Herring, *Writing Begins with the Breath*, 7.

Most of us likely live and serve somewhere between these extremes. This book and your accompanying field education experience will hopefully create a space for you to deepen your understanding and practice of ministry. Field education provides a starting point for developing and claiming pastoral voice. How you start in pastoral ministry sets patterns, either helpful or not, that you will use for many years.

Field education programs are not created equal. Indeed, requirements vary among field education programs. Students are usually granted considerable latitude with their learning goals and gain varying degrees of experience at their ministry sites. What I am proposing in this book does not eliminate the latitude that is typically given to students who are enrolled in a field education program. Instead, my proposals put students' interests and learning goals within the broad context of what constitutes the best and most complete preparation for imaginative, effective ministry in today's church and world.

Adult learning rightly looks to students to identify the areas of greatest resonance and need in their educational journey. But too often these learning goals are framed so myopically that their relationship to church and ministry seems marginal. To enroll in a field education program and not take note of the six possibilities for learning I have just outlined would be like strolling through a ripe orchard and not noticing the sweet fruit that is ready to be picked. To not address and explore these six areas of learning would be a strange and disembodied enterprise that would miss the point of experiential theological education. All of these areas get addressed in other parts of the curriculum, but in field education they are the curriculum.

As the preceding quote from Dykstra says, "It's a beautiful thing to see a good pastor at work." This book seeks to cultivate some of that beauty. By attending thoughtfully to the realities of your field education experience, you will begin to find and claim your pastoral voice. This book attempts to name some of the moments in your field education experience that will contribute to that process. The first chapter uses the story of Saul and David to describe the process of entertaining and then setting aside the voices of others in order to claim our own. Chapters two through six explore context, the Christian story, pastoral roles, personal identity, and systemic dynamics, respectively. Each of these chapters will name the issue, describe how your field education experience can explore it, present two fictional case studies that illustrate how this issue plays out, and then offer you ways to cultivate your pastoral voice relative to the issue.

It is important to note that the metaphor of voice occupies a prominent place in many pursuits, academic and otherwise. To "find voice" and to "claim voice" have become common ways of speaking about emerging perspectives, gifts, and identities.[9] We speak of teachers, community organizers, and others finding voice when their uniqueness gets expressed in the larger context of their work. Parents find voice as they understand and execute the particular ways they fulfill their parental roles and relate to their children. As well, the notion of finding voice has been attached to arenas like presidential politics, but not always in a positive way. On numerous occasions we have witnessed candidates with the seemingly perfect combination of preparation and pedigree take the stage only to reveal that they had nothing to say that really mattered.

When thinking about finding voice for a minister, the parallels of finding voice as a writer are especially interesting and informative. What distinguishes compelling writers from the rest of the pack is not subject-verb agreement. It is not an impressive vocabulary. It is not the writer's ability to develop characters or envision how a story can unfold, though these qualities are essential to good writing. What distinguishes compelling writers from everyone else is voice—their ability to authentically express themselves from some deep interior place that captures a slice of the human condition, holds before us some new way of being in the world, and leads us down some uncertain, yet inviting path. Writers who find such a voice move beyond the technical and into the experiential in ways that connect us to the life behind the words.

I am again reminded of the words of novelist Laraine Herring who says that deep, authentic writing does not come from our minds. Instead, she says, it arises "from our bodies, from our breath, and from our ability to remain solid in the places that scare us."[10]

Ministry is like that. Deep, authentic ministry arises from being present in those times and places that unnerve us. If we have held our own experiences at arm's length and avoided the exhilaration, fear, and ambiguity that accompanies those times, then our ministry may cruise above the realities of people's lives and not know their laughter and

---

9. Turner and Hudson, *Saved from Silence*, xii.

10. Herring, *Writing Begins with the Breath*, 6–7.

despair in any real way. What gets lost along the way is more than simply what we, as pastors, might have offered to those who are celebrating and hurting. The loss is also our own unrealized identity, and that loss will be felt in all the priestly, pastoral, and prophetic roles we perform, even if we continue to say and do many of the right things.

Theological field education provides a space for us to merge with what we are studying. Phoning it in does not work. If you have settled on the answers before starting out on the journey, then even your most eloquent voice will not compel anyone because your listeners will understand it as little more than disinterested conversation or will recognize it for what it is: theoretical calisthenics. As pastors, our performance is only credible when we have plumbed our deepest recesses and excavated things that animate and frighten us. The passion and focus that are discovered in this lifelong process of discovery gives shape and spirit to our faith and ministry. People in the congregation recognize pastors who have been and are on such a journey. Members of your congregation may not understand your journey, and they may have no interest in joining you, but they will take note of it and perhaps even decide to launch their own journey of faith as a result of the risks that you make evident in your own exploration.

Writer-activist Florida Scott Maxwell has a strong and certain voice. She once said, "You need only claim the events of your life to make yourself yours. When you truly possess all you have been and done, you are fierce with reality."[11] The opportunity to serve in ministry as one part of your seminary studies provides you with an opportunity to plumb your deepest recesses and excavate the things that energize and haunt you. In that process you may discover what tugs at your soul. And, along the way, you may discover a sustaining passion that provides you with a deep and steady engagement with ministry that, in the end, causes you, too, to be fierce with reality.

---

11. Maxwell, *Measure of My Days*, 42.

1

The Journey toward Voice

Reflections on Saul and David

Ask me whether what I have done is my life.[1]

—WILLIAM STAFFORD

THE POET WILLIAM STAFFORD writes:

> Some time when the river is ice ask me
> mistakes I have made. Ask me whether
> what I have done is my life. Others
> have come in their slow way into
> my thought, and some have tried to help
> or to hurt: ask me what difference
> their strongest love or hate has made."[2]

"Ask me," Stafford says, "Ask me whether what I have done is my life." These haunting words imply that a person can do many things, and all of them taken together still might not add up to a life. Or they may add up to somebody's life, but not our own.

---

1. Stafford, "Ask Me," 56.
2. Ibid.

The poet reminds us that others have a say in how we understand ourselves. We may get the final word about the shape and character of our lives, if we work hard enough at it, but we arrive at our identity in relationship to other people, places, and events. That experience is frustrating and clarifying, complicating, and transforming. Without engaging that experience it is unlikely we will ever understand our own personal identity or discover our pastoral voice.

Consider how that clarifying experience plays out in the story of Saul and David found in 1 Sam 17:31–40. This account is frequently referenced as the story of David and Goliath, and rightly so. But within that larger narrative is an exchange between David and Saul. This exchange describes the kind of interior sorting out that occurs when a person is held up for public examination.

Every morning and every evening, for forty days, Goliath emerges from his camp and calls out for a worthy opponent. Across the way, fear envelopes Saul and the Israelites. The stakes are high. The losers will become the servants of the winners.

David, to whom we were introduced in 1 Samuel 16 when he worked as a music therapist to ease Saul's tormented soul, becomes the unlikely opponent for Goliath. David is, after all, a youthful and handsome shepherd boy who is seemingly more comfortable playing his instrument, bearing Saul's armor, and running errands than engaging in battle.

With the Israelites running for cover in response to Goliath's thunderous challenge, David announces that the giant's defiance of the living God will not stand. David then inquires about what gain he might personally realize if he were victorious over Goliath, foreshadowing David's complex interests and motives.

Certain that the young boy does not have a chance in a fight with Goliath, Saul tries to discourage David. But David replies by building an impromptu resume that cites the lambs that he has rescued and the lions and bears he has killed while working as a shepherd. How much more difficult could fighting Goliath be, he asks, especially because he has the unequivocal promise that God will be with him?

The conversation between Saul and David is brief, but it reveals that David's identity quest is under way. The four movements of this exchange create a framework for our own personal and pastoral discovery.

SAUL GIVES HIS ARMOR TO DAVID

We pass on what is at our disposal. This is what Saul did. "Here, David, take my armor."

We humans give many things to each other over the course of our lives. This stuff that we give each other—and stuff isn't a technical term, but in some cases it's the most polite term—comes in the form of expectations, signals of approval and disapproval, views of the world as being either a safe or hostile place, patterns to follow, prejudices to adopt or reject, possibilities to pursue, woundedness that we want somebody else to feel, lines not to cross, and dreams that can and cannot be considered. Beneficial or harmful, all of this stuff cries out for us to become aware of it and reflect upon it, lest it become a Goliath-like monster that rears its ugly head at the most inopportune times.

Many people give things to their ministers—effusive encouragement, generous support, expectations for the minister and her family, models for ministry, personal issues of their own, or brokenness from church fights that seems to carry no expiration date. Without some careful processing of what is already going on in our lives, pastors may well hand the worst of those things to the people around them in their interactions with the congregation.

Moreover, these gifts may not be as helpful to the receiver as the giver imagines. Pastors and congregations are notorious for making assumptions about each other that dishonor one another and undermine their relationship. These assumptions can be found along a continuum between direct, explicit communications and tacit, insidious equivocations. For example, a congregation might, in effect, say the following to a new pastor:

"Here, Dana, we've got this booming pulpit voice left over from our previous pastor. It's how every great preacher sounds and you can have it! Go ahead, try it out for us."

Or, "Here, Pat, we've got this social gospel theology stored in the recesses of our congregational memory and have been waiting for someone who can dust it off and start injecting it back into all our discussions. Go ahead, this will fit perfectly. We can't wait to hear it coming out of your mouth!"

Or, "Here, Lindsey, we've got the ghost of another minister roaming these halls who thought that the reign of God depended on weekly fellowship dinners and nightly committee meetings. We aren't sure what you do all week, but we thought you might like to try these ideas on for size. We love a casserole-eating, detail-obsessed pastor and we will love you, too, once you start wearing this particular suit of pastoral priorities."

Of course, congregations also give gifts of infinite value and deep encouragement to their pastor. People articulate possibilities for a ministry that we, as pastors, may never have thought of or may not have considered doing. Indeed, an individual's call to ministry often emerges in moments when a congregation entrusts a particular aspect of ministry to that person, and through the experience of performing that ministry that individual's passions and gifts emerge. Through reflection and, in many cases, the affirmation that follows such an experience may cause that person to take pause and consider exploring the vocation of ministry more fully.

Some gifts that aid in developing our pastoral identity may perplex us when we first receive them. I can recall receiving such a gift when I was in my teenage years. It seemed like a small thing one Sunday when Mrs. Williams, an older woman in my home church, handed me a book her Sunday school class had been studying. "I thought you might be interested in this," she told me. I thanked her, but I couldn't imagine why she was giving me that book or what it had to do with my life. Over time I came to realize the gift wasn't so much the book. In fact, I don't even remember its title. But I came to see this small gift as being an invitation to think about a life path and, in that regard, this gift had quite a bit to do with my life. Mrs. Williams seemed to be aware of my likely vocational path before I was, and so she invited me to live in its possibility.

Theological field education puts you in a position to start receiving these many gifts—the good, the bad, and the ugly—so that you can begin sorting through them. It's a gift to be asked to preach on the first Sunday of Advent. It's also a gift to be given responsibility for the church's annual health fair and to coordinate ministry with men and women who are homeless. And it is still another gift to be invited to lead a study that encourages people to understand how their faith informs and interprets the rest of their lives. A congregation with capacity and willingness to provide as many of these gifts as possible will greatly benefit your quest for finding your pastoral voice.

DAVID TRIES ON SAUL'S ARMOR

The second move in this story comes when David did what many of us do when we are given a new thing—he tried it out. David put on Saul's armor and walked around in it.

In his book *Dreams from My Father*, then Harvard Law Review president Barack Obama powerfully describes his own challenges of trying to walk around with the gifts he'd been given. His gifts were not just the one personal story he inherited from his birth, but they were a convergence of a complicated set of stories that became even more complicated as he grew up.

Places as varied as Hawaii, Indonesia, Southern California, Chicago, and Kenya influenced Obama's life trajectory. He was shaped by a diverse group of people—grandparents from the Luo tribe in Kenya on one side of the family and a Kansan grandfather and a Cherokee grandmother of Scottish/English stock on the other. Factors of race, geography, culture, and familial status collided almost daily in Obama's life.

Obama was born to an American woman and a Kenyan man. His other family members and friends lived around the world and brought into his life an array of expectations, questions, prejudices, and possibilities. Obama describes looking into other people's lives and their narratives for clues about how his own life might fit together. He reports that on several occasions this approach not only intensified his confusions, but also increased the uncertainty of the people around him who, themselves, were already unclear about how best to relate to him. In one conversation, his friend Ray replies to one of Obama's comments with the simple line: "Speak for yourself." Silence ensued as Obama realized that he had no clear idea about who his own self was.[3]

For four hundred and fifty pages Obama's book begs the simple question, "Who am I?" In chapter after chapter Obama undertakes an identity quest that winds its way through expectations, disillusionment, questions, surprises, revelations, and reunions. And it is not until he visits Kenya, the land of his father, do some of the threads of his life begin to form a pattern that is understandable to him and, ultimately, empowers him.

That "trying on" experience is at the heart of your field education experience. This experience is designed to help you recognize the personal stories and events that have formed you. This process is meant to help you

3. Obama, *Dreams from My Father*, 82.

learn about the different models for effective ministry, watch seasoned pastors fulfilling those roles, and to try on and walk around in some of those roles yourself.

Breadth of experience in a ministry site will allow you to try out various models, approaches, and styles for conducting an effective ministry. Remember that David did not size up Saul's armor without trying it on. He did not say, "I'm sorry Saul, but I can just tell that's going to be a little short in the sleeves. And that helmet looks much too tight." Likewise, we should not make guesses about ministry. Students must walk around in pastoral roles long enough to entertain thoughts of filling them in the long term. And, in this way, the field education experience provides students with essential experience that allows them to clarify, confirm, and challenge their vocational path.

Interests and gifts arise in surprising areas as a result of this "trying on." I can think of a number of students who absolutely could not imagine themselves in the pulpit—that is until the first time they preached before a congregation. Afterward, they could not imagine not getting the opportunity to preach on a regular basis. It's also true that the first preaching experience leads others to realize that the pulpit does not have a compelling claim on their lives.

The lived experience of ministry brings our questions and concerns into sharper focus. Through this lived process, excuses that had allowed us to dismiss possibilities get revisited. Evidence mounts in this or that direction that, in turn, gives clarity and conviction to our call. Those wonderful moments occur when we start trying on and sorting out roles, responsibilities, styles, and ways of being in ministry.

In the field education program at the seminary where I serve, students develop a Personal Thick Description,[4] which asks them to identify significant people, events, and circumstances that have shaped their lives both positively and negatively. This exercise helps students explore their lives in such a way that they become more aware of what baggage they carry and how it might impact the development of their pastoral identity. Through this process, students gain insight into how their own identity quest has unfolded to that point, and why.

---

4. More will be said about the Personal Thick Description in chapter five.

DAVID PUTS SAUL'S ARMOR DOWN

In the third move, we are told that David puts down Saul's armor because he is not used to it. Something about it did not fit. It was not authentic to David's life, at least to that point.

Congregations often struggle to set aside things that do not fit with their gifts, vocation, tradition or context, whether it is a congregational event, a ministry program, or a mission initiative to the wider community. This is true even when a particular ministry emphasis clearly has outlived its usefulness and effectiveness. The same can be said of many ministers, who are so eager to please and be well liked that they find it difficult to lay down personal characteristics or models for ministry that simply are not authentic expressions of who they are. Because ministers have difficulty with saying "no," expectations in the congregation can mount to the point that ministers find themselves attempting to be all things to all people. The inevitable result is that these ministers end up being nothing to anybody, including themselves. What's more, these expectations are often self-imposed. This is because we, as ministers, frequently ask more of ourselves than what others ask of us. Whatever the source of these expectations, we too often try to fulfill every one of them, barely pausing to think about the consequences of gaining the whole world while losing our individual souls in the process.

Few moments are more sobering than when we, as ministers, recognize that we cannot fully embrace a call to ministry without encountering some losses and setting some things aside. Some losses include the following, for example:

- A cherished innocence about one's faith and theology may be lost as we explore what we believe, attempt to defend our views, and develop new skills of interpretation and understanding that are necessary for pastoral work.

- The social network of family and friends who, prior to us joining the ministry, lent support and granted us standing among a particular group of people or particular place.

- A prior vocational familiarity that helped us make sense of the world. As exciting as pursuing a call to ministry can be, it is difficult to leave known, satisfying work for what is unknown and uncertain.

- Pastoral and church models that influenced us to consider ministry in the first place. While aspiring ministers may thank God for the encounters that they had with effective pastors and vibrant communities of faith, these new ministers may not recognize that the vitality of these faith communities probably grew out of some context-specific realities that may never come to pass in their own ministry.

And consider, too, examples of unattractive things that hinder our journey toward voice, and so cry out to be put aside:

- Our own internal voices that persistently tell us we are not good enough, or smart enough, or gifted enough to be in ministry. Each of us encounters enough obstacles along the way that there is no need to discredit ourselves, too.

- The residue of toxic relationships and situations cause us to be more tentative than we otherwise might be. Naming these experiences is an important first step toward recovery, but some individuals among us may require therapy in order to fully lay them aside.

- External, formal voices that carry significant authority may stand in the way of our journey to ministry. An individual who makes a gut-wrenching decision to leave a church tradition may be held up by these voices. However, such an individual may have found that being faithful to the God who called him or her means that they must set aside a much-loved church and find a new family of faith. And so this individual embarks on a long and difficult journey to find voice.

- Other people's scripts and patterns that define, discourage, disapprove, and demean us. Those scripts distract us and undermine our efforts for as long as we pay attention to them.

Until we name and work through some of these losses it is unlikely we will develop a compelling voice. And yet, putting anything down—attractive or unattractive—is difficult. This is especially true when it comes to the safest voices and styles in ministry. As Herring puts it, "If there's nothing at stake for the author, there won't be enough energy to sustain a longer project."[5] Or as African-American poet and critic Michael Datcher says, "Authentic writing will have fallout."[6] If there's nothing at stake for

---

5. Herring, *Writing Begins with Breath*, 18.

6. Datcher, quoted in Herring, *Writing Begins with Breath*, 15.

pastors, there won't be energy enough to sustain the work. If ministry is authentic, it will have fallout. There will be losses.

What are we willing to set aside to be ourselves? What are we willing to lay down in order to give authentic expression to the mysteries and possibilities that stir our souls? It is risky business to tell the stories of faith through our own genuineness and to participate in the purposes of God without hedging our bets. But what else can we do? We who are in ministry either put ourselves out there in all our glory and vulnerability or we become something like religious technicians to whom nothing about this life and world ultimately matters.

This quest for authentic voice is not an easy process, but without this level of introspection we are unlikely to arrive at a full-throated pastoral voice. Field education provides opportunities in real time and in a specific location that allows you to take risks that, in turn, will bring your pastoral identity into clearer focus. The clarification of your pastoral journey may begin within the bounds of a particular semester of field education, but the process of discovery looks well beyond the horizon of any academic calendar. The work is ongoing. During your time as a seminary student, you may lay down some obvious things, but you should know that ministry's vocational path continues to fork as long as you are on it, and you will be confronted repeatedly with decisions that ask you to embrace this and lay down that.

DAVID ENGAGES HIS OWN LIFE

In his fourth and last move, David claims what is consistent with his own life. David leaves Saul's helmet, armor, and sword laying on the ground around him, and instead picks up things from his own life—his staff, sling, and five smooth stones from his shepherd's bag.

David's warrior impulse and his grab for power ultimately consume him. But, for the purposes of this discussion, let us focus only on David as he takes up something from his life as a shepherd. Like David who seeks comfort and confidence in what he knows, we too discover our pastoral voice not just by rejecting the models of others, but by taking up the familiar and trusted things that are already in our own lives.

In her extensive writing about mainline churches and their leadership, Diana Butler Bass notes the correlation between the self-understanding of ministers and the vitality of congregations. Effective clergy leaders know their story and lead with it. Bass writes, "Some people know their stories and tell them well but live without intentional connection to those stories; others simply experience the quotidian life with no reflection on larger stories of meaning. In vital mainline churches, leaders knew their stories and lived them—thus turning the power of narrative into a source of and resource for change."[7]

Bass draws a distinction between telling stories and living by them. Leading with our personal stories is about doing more than regurgitating the unrestrained, unstudied events of the preceding week. Instead, effective leaders probe an experience for what is significant about it, and then connect its importance to their lives and their ministry.

In my church tradition, laypersons take major leadership roles at the Lord's Table. One of the common arguments in our free worship is whether or not our elders should prepare their prayers ahead of time or if they should "pray from the heart" while at the table. However, this argument provides a false dichotomy. For, the only way to pray from the heart is to spend time becoming aware of what is in one's heart—one must reflect on its hope and sorrow, and then convey these sentiments through a prayer that is the true overflow of what lives within us. Those who want our elders to pray from the heart confuse that practice with "shooting from the hip." In the role of both pastors and lay leaders, we have the glad and humbling responsibility when leading public worship to offer words that address God from the deep places of faith and experience. In any event, a good bit of preparation is required to undertake such a holy task.

In their work *Know Your Story and Lead with It*, Richard L. Hester and Kellie Walker-Jones urge ministers to step outside the disorienting experience of living in others' preferred stories. These writers provide a process that is informed by narrative therapy theory whereby we become more aware of the stories that shape our lives, put aside stories that wield disproportionate and unhealthy power over our lives, and begin to understand, author, and claim practices and patterns that are born of our own thought and priorities.[8] Authority, in part, is born in the opportunity to author our own story, or in this case, our authentic expression of the church's ministry.

7. Bass, "Living the Story."
8. Hester and Walker-Jones, *Know Your Story*, 26.

Jesus blessed the crowd on the hillside with the announcement, "You are the light of the world."[9] He continued the thought by urging those gathered to "let your light shine before others."[10] The light that shines upon us and through us is the light that illumined the formless void at the dawn of creation. It is the light that we witness in Jesus, a light that darkness has not overcome. We will reflect that light differently from person to person, minister to minister. Jesus told the people around him, "Let *your* light shine." In the extravagant giftedness in the family of God, your particular light and my particular light will differ. I cannot shine your light anymore than you can shine my light. Taken as a whole, however, your light and mine are complementary, just as the parts of the body work together in wholeness.

This journey of discovering pastoral voice is an exciting one. It is through this process that you will engage in your own life, and in so doing find your voice. The life and work of Beverly Harrison, who taught for many years at Union Seminary in New York, provides an excellent example of this journey to pastoral voice. Harrision describes her experience of assuming a voice that, at least initially, "was overly determined by others rather than one that articulated an authentic reflection of her own questions."[11] As a result, her male colleagues in ministry admired her, but primarily because she fit into their preconceived notions about what would constitute the nature and focus of her ministry, namely, a woman whose work would be limited to the area of Christian education. When she began a campus ministry, her male colleagues strongly supported her, but did so because she continued to function in a model that they felt at home with. She found compelling female role models, but even as they helped her they also hindered her efforts to assess her distinctive gifts and kindle her particular passions and interests.[12]

As Harrison began to work with female seminary students who were sorting out their identities in the context of conflicting expectations, she was confronted with how much authority she had given the external voices around her. Through the process of rethinking these issues, she gained new clarity about her vocational path and understood the importance of

9. Matt 5:14.

10. Matt 5:16.

11. Harrison, "Keeping Faith in A Sexist Church," 206–34.

12. Ibid.

personal authenticity in finding her voice. Taking up what was most consistent to her life, she advocated widely for justice and fairness.[13] You can see the moves in David's life playing out in much of Harrison's journey. Harrison received numerous gifts in the form of models and expectations for ministry. Just as David did, she tried on a number of those models and expectations. Then, though it was not without difficulty, she put aside those that were not congruent with her own self-understanding and her understanding of the gospel. Finally, she engaged the rich depths of her own life and found an authentic expression for her ministry. *Finding Voice* seeks to guide you through a similar process of sorting, clarifying, and claiming your pastoral identity.

SUMMING UP AND GETTING STARTED

A vigorously reflective self is necessary for a pastoral voice to emerge. Your field education provides space, companions, and experiences to surface your truest self. Theological field education seeks to aid your discovery and nurture your voice by putting you in situations that will challenge, clarify, and confirm how you understand yourself and your vocation. The intent of field education is to provide a sufficient array of pastoral experiences and moments of reflection so that you can begin to recognize, trust, and take up what stirs in the deep places of your soul. In the process, you will discover within God's extravagant diversity your authentic voice for the gospel's claims. As a result, your preaching, congregational leadership, care for those in crisis, and work for fairness in the community can become a genuine expression of your experience of the faith and your particular giftedness.

13. Ibid.

2

Understanding Where You Are

The miracle is not walking on water.
The miracle is to walk on the green earth in the present moment.[1]

—Thich Nhat Hanh

WHY CONTEXT MATTERS

Imaginative and effective ministry requires that you understand where you are and what goes on around you. This chapter explores how pastoral voice arises when you engage with the particularities of your immediate context and with the shifts and trends that are afoot in the broader culture.

We often want to conduct our spiritual journeys without any specific context. We want to eliminate any and all distractions that might get in our way, often including the people and practices of a community of faith. In doing so, we sidestep anything that might complicate or muddy our quest for the purest faith experiences. Seeking spiritual moments in this way frees us from the interferences that infringe on other parts of our lives—the difficult individuals, stifling traditions, stunning hypocrisies, divisive politics, narrow-minded policies, and burdensome processes.

1. Hanh, *Touching Peace*, 1.

But it is a profound error to seek the presence and ways of God in the abstract, free from any commitments to a given group or a specific place.

Thomas Merton reminds us that God is revealed in the middle of conflict and contradiction. Merton goes so far as to say that this contradiction is required for our own creativity.[2] We may understandably seek escape from the overwhelming complexity of life that is all around us, but, again, ministry does not occur in the abstract or the theoretical. Nor does ministry—or the faith that undergirds it—encourage or condone escape from the realities of our lives. Ministry happens in the messiness of contradictory stories and in fluid, multi-layered situations. Ministry occurs alongside people grappling with an assortment of questions, loyalties, needs, and dreams. An understanding of context helps each of us connect our particular lives to a particular place. This contextualized understanding then provides the framework within which we live, work, play, and pursue relationships. Ministry facilitates conversations that help individuals and congregations sort out matters of faith in relationship to all manners of daily responsibilities, desires, and challenges. A coherent and purposeful wholeness emerges when the many parts of our lives continually speak to each other.

Jesus came into this world not as an idea or proposition or theory, but as a baby born in radical particularity. Regardless of how much we want to romanticize Mary's pregnancy, or the earthy collection of animals and shepherds that surrounded the manger, the human life of Jesus begins in the messiness of childbirth and plays out in the promise and peril of peasants who are trying to survive under oppressive Roman rule in the first century.

Context has shaped the Christian story at every turn. Paul's letter to the Philippians, for instance, grew out of his warm relationship with a certain group of Christians living in Philippi in the middle part of the first century. Paul names specific women, Euodia and Syntyche, who played key roles in that young congregation; and he speaks to issues and circumstances being faced by the particular Christian community living there.

Context applies to more than biblical figures, of course. The life and work of Sojourner Truth is such an example. She was born into slavery near the end of the eighteenth century; and that reality became the context for her life's work. In the midst of an embarrassingly brutal time in

2. Montaldo, *A Year with Thomas Merton*, 14.

American history, she experienced God's claim on her life by saying "the truth calls me." At that point, she changed her name to Sojourner Truth and over the course of the next forty years, until her death in 1883, she became a compelling advocate for freedom, fairness, and nonviolence.

The life and works of a contemporary theologian like Rosemary Radford Ruether also illustrates the importance of personal context. Ruether's feminist theology developed in the context of a faith that had too long been dominated by masculine language, images, and perspectives. She sought more inclusive dialogue by articulating a broader understanding of God and by calling attention to the ways sexism fractured creation and communities.

Context shaped the understanding and efforts of these people and, in turn, these people shaped the contexts in which they did their work. Today, as we participate in the Christian story, our context shapes the church, and the church influences, at least some of the time, our context.

THE INFLUENCE OF CONTEXT AND CONGREGATION UPON EACH OTHER

Let's consider the former situation first, that of context influencing the church. A context and its accompanying attitudes, norms, and practices shape a church's life and witness. Cultural norms from beyond a church affect life within that church. The formality or informality of the meetings in a given church likely reflects the spirit with which things are done in the broader community. Communities that take a conservative approach to finances likely will have churches that do the same. Communities that suppress difference and conflict will often be home to churches that deal with difference and conflict in the same manner. People who hold positions of power in the community frequently, for good or ill, hold positions of power in the church.

These are particularly interesting times for the American church. It is not difficult to identify cultural norms that run counter to the Christian gospel: greed, destruction, and hatred, just to name a few. Indeed, to some extent every congregation finds itself in a paradoxical relationship with its context. Church congregations can play a critical role in challenging the dehumanizing practices and forces that violate the life and teachings of Jesus and tear apart human community, but even the most prophetic congregations often discover ways in which they have chosen to fit into the local landscape rather than to challenge it. Conversely, even those congregations that for the most part identify rather closely with the broader culture demonstrate some counter-cultural commitments and practices. Simply put, the relationship between context and congregation can be very complex.

Nancy Ammerman and her colleagues write about this relationship: "Dominant issues are those that are perceived to be in nearly everyone's interests. When religion backs dominant issues, it is likely to be more successful than when it backs minority issues—those that benefit only a small group or are perceived to be divisive in the community."[3] Perhaps this is why church growth strategies often include the advice that instructs congregations to stay clear of controversial issues.

When the goal of congregations is to measure themselves according to cultural success, then they might decide to keep the lid on conversations that address some of the most pressing issues for that time and place. These congregations are merely taking their cues from the environment in which they find themselves and, in so doing, reinforce the cultural, racial, and economic divisions of the wider society. Their desire to be seen as good citizens of the community causes them to adopt the prevailing norms and practices, even when those norms and practices stand in direct opposition to the gospel. Lost is the prophetic distance and edge necessary for that church to identify with and act from the center of the gospel's larger truth.

On the other hand, congregations have the capacity to engage and influence their contexts and occasionally they do so. Some congregations adopt faith positions that encourage members to work in opposition to prevailing, life-diminishing patterns of the larger culture. As followers of Jesus, we live out a dual citizenship: we must engage in the larger culture, but we must do so while proclaiming, embodying, and working for the shalom that God intends for all creation. In doing so, we often put ourselves at odds with the impulses and practices of a local context and the broader culture.

Congregations influence their contexts in various ways, though some of these influences are terribly difficult to quantify. For example, a welcoming, hospitable congregation that bears witness in its own life

---

3. Ammerman et al, *Studying Congregations*, 69.

and practices to a loving, inclusive God can at least give pause to a big-oted wider community, and may even soften some of its prejudices. A congregation that fosters vigorous and honest conversations that matter to people's lives will be looked to as a model when the community under-takes difficult and controversial issues. A congregation whose ministries are expressed in humility and mutuality, as opposed to a triumphalistic harbinger of a narrow and rigid truth, will nurture respect and neigh-borliness in the broader context. Perhaps the most compelling of all is how the participants of a congregation live among and relate to the wider community. They may not share their faith explicitly or advertise their church openly, but the joy and hope that overflow from their encounters with God and each other through their congregation will be felt as they move about their town or city.

In addition to the general ways that the presence of a life-giving congregation can influence its context, numerous situations call for well-organized and highly concrete direction action. For instance, a congre-gation located near an Army base might become a Peace Church, offer public forums on Just War principles, and seek to live more by love and reconciliation than fear and revenge. Another church might decide to protest the way its city government abandons the people in certain areas of town and, in the process of taking action to right this wrong, influence city budget and zoning decisions through regular involvement of city planning meetings. Still another church might picket the school district until it hires a more diverse faculty.

A particular church can rise to this measure of faithfulness, but the odds of doing so diminish greatly if that church has invested time and energy fitting into the broader culture, suppressing conflict, and allying itself only with what is deemed respectable, popular, and uncontroversial. Christians living in tension with local norms and broader cultural trends must constantly sort out what is life-giving and what is death-dealing. This way of living causes each individual and congregation to side with, and participate in, that which gives life.

Context presses each church beyond broad themes and hypothetical positions and places them into a realm of specifics by which that church will define its priorities and practices. It is there that opportunities for ministry surface. Leadership choices are then considered by the congre-gation, and then interpreted into becoming something that the congrega-tion devotes itself to or not. Because most congregations cannot engage with every situation and issue, members and leaders must identify what issues or concerns in their immediate context fits within their particular congregational calling. Likewise, they must trust that some other congregation will accept these other concerns as its calling. A minister must have thorough familiarity with the religious landscape of a given place. This familiarity is essential to effectively living in the tension of the church's particular context. Such a church speaks to a community as a part of that community, even in those instances when what needs to be said may not be wholly welcomed.

RECOGNIZING CONTEXTUAL DIFFERENCES

Differences among some contexts are so pronounced that almost anyone can recognize them. A congregation situated in an arts district of New York City likely will differ from a church located in the shadow of a major military installation in northern Alabama. The life of an inner-city church in a crime-ridden area will have different rhythms, concerns, and opportunities than most suburban neighborhood congregations. A farming community with a rapidly declining population base will have a different set of concerns than will a church at the center of a quickly sprawling development on the edge of a growing city. Context matters. One context is not better than another. Simply, each context embodies particular opportunities and challenges.

The contextual differences noted in the examples in the preceding paragraph would be hard to miss. Other differences, however, are more subtle. Pastoral leaders who do not stay current with their contexts often miss what is evolving all around them. This is especially the case with congregations that have turned in upon themselves in the well-intentioned but misguided effort to survive as a church. It is unlikely that a congregation will survive, much less flourish, without being attuned to its immediate context and the major shifts occurring in the broader culture. Ministers sometimes ignore these changes in order to continue predetermined leadership plans, or they make erroneous and often arrogant assumptions about life in a particular place, or they ignore its interesting distinctiveness, and in so doing miss nuanced contextual differences that pose fascinating possibilities for ministry.

Identifying contextual differences and their implications between locations is easier when we use polarities like New York City and northern Alabama. A more difficult task is to pick up on the variations of life among churches in the same area, such as in a small town wherein many congregations can be found. The broader context may be identical for these churches in that small town setting, where spoken and unspoken pressures demand conformity. Not only do individuals bend toward an acceptable, nonthreatening sameness, such environments also create a fairly narrow range of church expressions from which few congregations will stray. While it makes sense that congregations in essentially the same context would look and act in similar ways, this also means that churches often appear to be more influenced by contextual concerns than by gospel expectations. Context is this reason why churches, on occasion, back away from the energizing values and practices at the heart of their faith traditions. They do so in order not to be seen as being too radical or too far outside the mainstream of their particular place.

Not everyone is convinced that context matters. People who do not appreciate the significance of contextual issues tend to either disregard local realities or disconnect from them entirely. These people may strip places of their particularities and then impose generalities on every setting, whether it is Boston or the bayou area. Each of us can easily experience this flattening out of American culture by walking into a box store or chain restaurant: we are, by design, meant to experience these places in the same way every time, regardless of location. To find the really interesting expressions of a place requires a person to adventurously probe the life that lurks in the more out-of-the-way spaces. If cultural sameness is all that person wants to find, then he or she can easily find examples of it. In one sense, people experience comfort and acceptance from the sameness in congregations, especially through patterns and rituals that convey God's presence and healing wherever those people may find themselves. However, because the Christian story is highly particularized, the most compelling encounter of the faith will occur when the gospel intersects with the realities of life that individuals and congregations deal with every day in their contexts.

Alternatively, people who do not believe that local context matters may be unaware, intentionally or not, of the stories that have shaped life in a particular place. Admittedly, we, in general, would like to forget some of those stories. Who wants to remember the devastation of Hurricane Katrina on the Gulf Coast, or rehearse the riots of South Central Los Angeles, or revisit the dramatic decline of small towns across much of the United States? But these stories tell us all something about a particular location and who we are as observers—and who the participants are as individuals. Losses are real and painful to recall, but forgetting these stories of loss and hardship disconnects us from life as it really is. Indeed, forgetting these losses causes us undue guilt and deepens despair. By contrast, losses that are voiced and grieved permit newness.[4] We easily understand why the preference is to forget some stories, but it seems that even the "good" ones—the interesting, fascinating, renewing stories—go largely unnoticed and untold.

Sometimes, we do not know the story of our own particular place, and exhibit little interest in learning it. In her book *Dakota*, Kathleen Norris describes how people in the small South Dakota town of Lemmon were unfamiliar with key stories that continued to shape their shared lives. This book is an unflinching look at the profound joys, subtle callings, and harsh limitations of life in a defined setting. But it is the subtitle, *A Spiritual Geography*, that captures the work that falls to pastoral leaders. Once again, context matters.

Contextual appreciation is a difficult endeavor for many ministers. As ministers, we may well encounter stories that we wish we had not learned. These stories also can test us and ask us to engage deeply in the complexity of a given place, for better or worse. No doubt, it is easier for a minister to give into the social and economic influences that want to sweep aside the history of a place and remake it in the image of the least common denominator. And in so doing, a minister feels he or she has resolved an unpleasant truth. But the work of ministry is not to resolve tensions—and surely it is not to flatten them out. Rather, the work of ministry is to engage conflicts honestly and work creatively with their opportunities and possibilities. As Norris says about life in *Dakota*, "I make no attempt in this book to resolve the tensions and contradictions I find in the Dakotas between hospitality and insularity, change and

---

4. Brueggemann, *Journey to the Common Good*, 87.

inertia, stability and instability, possibility and limitation, between hope and despair, between open hearts and closed minds."[5]

What Norris says about the Dakotas is true, to one degree or another, of all the places where we attempt ministry. Indeed, a careful study of context alerts us to the stories that shape life in that place. Every place, just like every person, embodies inconsistencies and complexities that can be mind-boggling and immensely frustrating for everyone involved. Those seemingly contradictory realities often are overlooked, ignored or denied because congregational leaders often view them as inconveniences or threats rather than possibilities. Pastors and congregations tend to force those conflicts and contradictions underground by focusing on easier problems and situations, even though those problems and situations offer no new learning and little likelihood of a way forward. The result is that life gets reduced to thin narratives that are incapable of generating much joy and adventure.

To learn a place through contextual study—and to learn ministry through contextual education—does not ask you to resolve competing values and different priorities. Rather, it asks you to recognize the complexity of a place. You will make quick connections between some of the pieces. Others will not seem to fit together at all. This glimpse into the lived reality of the people around you is an opportunity for you to become more aware of the complexities of your own life.

If you are able to engage such complexities, a new life will emerge for you, which is only earned through candid reflection, honest discussion, and clearer thinking. Ministers who use and champion a process that allows people to freely speak the unspeakable about themselves and their place in a safe environment, especially in the context of the church, often discover that the barriers of shame, timidity, and uncertainty are rather low hurdles to overcome. And, once these barriers are overcome, a community can then begin to reclaim the richer, thicker, life-giving narratives that in turn provide perspective, energy, celebration, and purpose.

5. Ibid, 7.

LEARNING THE CONTEXT AROUND
THE CONGREGATION

In Bible courses, we read ancient accounts of people who grapple with God's presence and God's leading. We engage in these accounts of these people by paying close attention to language, genre, and message. In theology, we learn to articulate an understanding of God and God's purposes within given streams of a religious tradition. In history, we learn about the impact that various people, places, and events have had on the church's trajectory. In field education, we learn a place. How well we learn the exacting realities and influences of a place determines how fully present we will be in it, whether we will honor or debase that place, and what strategies for ministry and congregational life will be appropriate and effective.

A French proverb poses the question, "What is the last thing a fish realizes?" Groups discussing this arrive at answers that range from "That it has been hooked" to "That it cannot breathe out of water" to "That it is a fish." The aphorism reveals that the last thing a fish discovers is that it is in water. This is to say that even though the fish is surrounded by water constantly—or maybe because it is surrounded by water constantly—the fish can become rather oblivious to its context.

We do not pause often to consider context—like fish, we do not pay much attention to the water. Because of this, you may find it helpful to consciously consider the contexts that surround you. If you consider how each context influences the way you see the world, perhaps you might better understand your place in it. For example, what was your first context? Most would say that it was their family. What patterns, expectations, and attitudes have you adopted, modified, or rejected from your family of origin? Were there certain behaviors your family deemed acceptable but that your friends and their families did not tolerate? And vice versa? Where did your family draw the line drawn between sharing and personal privacy?

Another context that surrounds us constantly is the location where we live. Do you live in a rural area, a small town, the suburbs, or at the core of an urban area? What difference does that make in terms of the pace of life, or the diversity you encounter, or the freedom you feel you have to express your identity, values, and preferences? Do you live in a place that is valued by the larger community, or is your place one that seems to be abandoned and forgotten? How does living in the United States influence your thoughts and assumptions, and how might you think about certain decisions and actions if you lived in another country? How are your political, social, economic, and religious views influenced by the polarizing debates that might rage and seethe around you?

Another context to consider is the virtual community. Technology has eliminated the need for many face-to-face interactions. How does technology impact your shared life when you are working with others in public spaces on a common project? How do your relationships that develop via Facebook, Twitter, or other social networking sites compare with the relationships that you form when you meet others in the same bar or classroom or living room or fellowship hall? Has the nature of friendship changed? What are the implications for inter-generational communication? What is the effect of news being available 24/7?

Ronald Heifetz and his colleagues at the Harvard Business School describe how people develop default interpretations and then unknowingly apply them when discerning and making organizational decisions.[6] Without much awareness on our part, these defaults shape our attitudes and actions. We allow this to happen because defaults create a sense of familiarity and comfort in changing times, but defaults also blind us to problems and solutions that are worth exploring. Even when, at some level, we know things have changed—and over time, those changes can be significant—we invoke default interpretations to new situations and in so doing allow these interpretations to serve as the basis of our decisions. When pastors and congregations drift further and further from the current realities of their context, they offer ministries that the community experiences as irrelevant or disconnected from life as people know it.

For example, a certain era can become so engrained in society that we cannot recognize that times have changed. Many church organizational structures rely on an institutional loyalty that flourished in 1952, but that sort of loyalty is barely detectable in today's culture. And yet, many congregations today are still trying to build an organizational structure that is derived from that very different era. Even when some congregational leaders reflect on their personal and professional lives outside the church, recognizing that the "water" outside the church has changed, some strange disconnect occurs and they nonetheless reinforce the old defaults within the church.[7]

---

6. Heifetz, *Practice of Adaptive Leadership*, 63–67.

7. For a helpful discussion of this, see Hamm, *Recreating the Church*.

Once upon a time in history, change occurred roughly at the rate that an individual's hair turned gray. Change was easy enough to track. We might even miss some changes, to no real effect. Or we could even deny that change was happening. By contrast, change in the early part of the twenty-first century is said to be occurring at an exponential pace. Until this moment in time, many congregations that did not keep up with the gradual but steady change of prior decades could nonetheless survive. With change now happening at an exponential rate, many of these congregations feel like strangers in their native settings. This is a time that calls for pastors to think critically about what is changing and to discern what aspects of the change can be faithfully appropriated to congregational life and what aspects of it would compromise the core values of the gospel and the church. It is also a time that requires pastors to demonstrate an unusual degree of agility and nimbleness. Pastors who are comfortable with this rapid rate of change are a revitalizing source of energy to such congregations. At the same time, pastors who move too quickly or with insufficient explanation or inadequate pastoral sensitivity will likely meet with significant resistance. As established congregations develop nimbleness in their decision making and implementation of ministry initiatives, they can teach fast-forward ministers the necessary pastoral virtues of patience, presence, and context. That is why learning a place is an act of sustained attention, for both ministers and members of the congregation.

A word of warning is due here, however. While new pastors can bring a fresh set of eyes to a context and successfully lead established congregations in a process of discovery, such pastors must have a strong sense of self and call in order to withstand the onslaught of the enforcers of the default standards. Effective leaders in such situations identify obstacles to learning a place, and then work to identify and diminish each one.

Observing, Listening, Gathering, and Interpreting

To learn a place as it is—as opposed to accepting the popular default interpretations of it—requires that we engage in four aspects of research: observing, listening, gathering, and interpreting.[8] The following paragraphs highlight some distinguishing aspects of these four components.

8. Appendix A of this book discusses this research in more detail, and also includes particular resources, questions, and issues for readers to explore.

The first component for learning a place is observation. You will see things upon arrival at your ministry site that you may never see again in the same way. You will notice things about the area around the church that will eventually blend into the background after you have been there for any length of time at all. If you have been at your ministry site for a while, you need to reexamine the things you have grown accustomed to seeing and attempt to view them with fresh eyes. Whether you are new to your site or continuing work there, you should pay particular attention to things that others may take for granted. This sort of detailed observation requires that you invest your presence, time, and attention. Resist the temptation to walk directly from the parking lot into the church without taking time to consider the surroundings. Once outside of the church building engage the context with all your senses on full alert.

The second component for learning a place is listening. You must listen to what others tell about the area where the congregation is located. You are seeking perspectives to the question, "What is life like here?" You should talk one-on-one with people, some who are in the congregation and some from the wider community. Your aim is to come into contact and listen to people who have varying degrees of familiarity with the area around the church. These interviews will help you develop a sympathetic, discerning understanding of the congregation's context. This is what Thomas Edward Frank calls an "ethnographic disposition."[9] This effort will require mental space and stillness of soul on your part. It also will likely involve a certain discipline as you guide the conversations. Expect that the people in the congregation will want to talk about the congregation, not the area around it. For many people, the only time they are in the part of the town or city where their church is located is when they go to church for worship. You will, of course, want to hear their perspectives and opinions about the area. But such conversations also provide you with an opportunity to prompt them to look with fresh eyes upon things that for them are "hidden in plain view."

The third component for learning a place is gathering. Your task is to gather the historical, cultural, and demographic information of the place. Your local and seminary libraries likely contain a variety of books that tell the story of how a community was founded and evolved through the years. Most states and larger cities have at least one history or encyclopedia that

9. Frank, *Soul of the Congregation*, 72.

captures the pivotal figures and moments of its past.[10] Archival searches produce newspaper articles about area celebrations and conflicts. Also available are artistic and literary expressions that are native to the place. Books and journals include sections that capture what was influencing the cultural landscape of the place at a given time. For example, as I write this book, works like Thomas Friedman's *The World Is Flat* and Phyllis Tickle's *The Great Emergence* are enormously popular.

Demographic information, which is available from various sources on the World Wide Web, provides a wide range of data related to population groups and how they break out by gender, age, race, ethnicity, educational level, per capita income, percentage of home ownership, family makeup, and other relevant information. Some websites also provide glimpses into religious, political, and social preferences, which is particularly interesting information when we approach context in terms of a two-way street, whereby the church and the context influence each other. We undertake demographic studies after we have first observed and listened; not before, because demographic studies tend to reinforce the dominant view of a place and what we already see and hold to be true. And so we observe and listen prior to conducting the demographic study in order that we can know what questions to ask of it.

From these sources you will gain an appreciation for the changing landscape on which your church now finds itself. Not every congregation will engage each of the issues you discover, but many of these issues will at least be recognizable in a congregation. Your aim is to discover the ways in which your congregation has struggled with those issues already, or is presently struggling with them.

The fourth component for learning a place—after you have observed, listened, and gathered information—is to try to make sense of the information you have before you. Interpretative work is critical to a pastoral leader's ability to teach and lead. Through observing, listening, and gathering information, you will begin to form some opinions about the place where you have been called to do ministry. These informed opinions allow you an opportunity to stand back and see the patterns that have emerged and discover what areas require further investigation. The interpretative work will help you and the people in your congregation remain honest about the "water" that surrounds the church. As

10. An example of this for the city where I live is *The Encyclopedia of Indianapolis*.

noted earlier, some people tend to develop default interpretations that, as time goes by, they do not revisit frequently enough. Things change, but not everyone notices those changes. Or, if these individual's do not like the changes, they refuse to participate in the new community that is emerging, or pretend the changes never happened, or hope against hope that these changes will go away so that the former ways may return. Any plans for ministry are suspect when outdated information is employed in the process of addressing changes. A study conducted in this manner is not unlike hitting the Refresh button of a web browser in an effort to see things as they are in that moment, today. With what you have observed, heard, and gathered before you, you can begin the interpretative process by asking questions, clarifying information, and identifying consistencies and incongruences that you discovered during your research. Your informed opinions can then be useful in creating relevant actions that you and your congregation can take.

Anne Lamott tells her writing students that "knowledge of your characters emerges the way a Polaroid develops."[11] We live in the digital age, and so we are used to reviewing pictures on a camera's screen immediately after we take them. This is to say, many younger people today may not even recognize Lamott's metaphor. Once upon a time, Polaroid cameras spit out fuzzy photo paper upon which the seeds of the recently taken picture were germinating. People gently blew on the paper and waved it in the air to help the picture appear. At family gatherings, a coffee table would be lined with photo sheets in various stages of development, and people would gather around in anticipation to see what had been captured.

Learning a place is more like snapping pictures with the old one-step Polaroid cameras. The picture emerges over time and, just when we think we have a clear handle on life in that place, something else comes into clearer view. To learn a context is to understand how, in the words of Kentucky poet Wendell Berry, a particular community belongs to its place and how a livable life is constructed and experienced there.[12] At its best, the learning of a place results in you becoming a native to that place, not in the sense of being insular or provincial, but in the sense that you appreciate what is there besides you and your interests. In so doing, you might even begin to see yourself as being a part of that place.

11. Lamott, *Bird by Bird*, 44.

12. Berry, *Imagination in Place*, 61.

To learn a place and to love a place are two different things. We cannot really love a place without learning it. Apart from a careful, prayerful contextual analysis, we can only love the idea of a place in terms of its abstractions by way of our impositions. To love a place is to know its endearing qualities and its embarrassing foibles. Further, to love a place is to remain hopefully present to its nuanced and intermingling realities. Of course, any love carries implications for heartbreak. Your attachment to a community, even for a relatively brief field education experience, contains this possibility. If you have learned your context well, then you will discover the pain of that place and these pains will begin to feel like a burden of your own.

To learn about and love a place is to know and affirm some sense of the sacred in that place. We, as ministers, are more than census takers who collect data; we are more than sociologists who report trends; and we are more than historians who recount the story of a community. Pastoral leaders would be inhibited in their work without the efforts of census takers, sociologists, historians, and many others who contribute understanding and insight to the tasks of ministry. But our calling is to understand a place and interpret the presence, purposes, and possibilities of God in that place. We, as ministers, are situated in a community of faith that is attempting to make sense of the community around them; and as ministers we must hope to impact the community with the justice and mercy of Jesus. To do so, we should position ourselves at the intersection of the gospel and context, and then engage a mutually critical conversation between the two in order to understand what faithfulness requires of us at that moment. Without learning and loving the place of our ministry, it is unlikely that any of our plans or strategies for that place will ring true or bear fruit.

To learn a place is to know the truth of that place, and knowing the truth of a place is a key step in a minister's journey toward discovering a vital and focused pastoral identity. Moreover, you must ask yourself what the truth of a particular place calls forth in you.

HOW CONTEXT GIVES RISE TO PASTORAL VOICE: SOME CASE STUDIES

This section offers two case studies that show how the engagement with the immediate context of a congregation led the student ministers to reconsider the significance of context, to learn key elements about what life is like in the area around their congregations, and to think more intentionally about implications for the development of their pastoral voice and for the congregation's ministry.

Bruce and Harris Memorial Church

Bruce grew up in a rural area that was, racially, almost exclusively white. Race was rarely discussed while growing up in his Caucasian household. He had two African-American classmates in his high school graduating class of 160 students. The first time he studied under an African-American teacher was during his senior year of college.

When Bruce decided to attend seminary, and began looking for a field education ministry site, he considered three possibilities: two were strong, Anglo congregations—one suburban and one urban; and the third was a small African-American church of another denomination in a neighborhood known for its crime, drug trade, and violence. Only the smaller African-American congregation, Harris Memorial, contacted him for an interview. The position would entail some leadership responsibilities in worship, regular teaching of an adult Sunday school class, occasional pastoral care opportunities, and management of the church's community center two days a week.

Rev. Martina, the pastor at Harris Memorial, gave Bruce a map of the neighborhood and asked him to walk the area on two different days. She instructed Bruce to record on the map what he saw and what he felt at various points during his walk. Bruce completed the assignment and made a few extra notes about what he had observed.

Bruce was unprepared for Rev. Martina's first question about the experience. "So Bruce," the pastor began, "you have walked our neighborhood twice. What have you learned about yourself?"

Bruce thought that the pastor had misspoken, but the waiting expression on Rev. Martina's face indicated that she had asked exactly the question she wanted to ask.

"What did I learn about myself?" Bruce was prepared to discuss abandoned houses, street-corner business transactions, a domestic dispute that had spilled out into a front yard, and the worst streets and sidewalks he had ever seen. He had even talked to two other ministers in the neighborhood, both of whom had helped Bruce understand that usually the only white males to visit this neighborhood are police officers or bill collectors.

After a considerable pause, Bruce responded. "I grew up in a small, almost all white community. But even though I did not interact regularly with people of other races, I still thought I understood their lives, you know, their opportunities and their challenges. I was convinced that I did not have a racist bone in my body, even though I had never really had the chance to test that. Now, well, I don't know. I hope I am not racist, but I know I am a part of a system that is terribly broken. I was scared to death walking around this neighborhood, and when I got over my fear I became very sad. Not only have I never been in a place like this, I either didn't know, or didn't want to know, such places exist."

"This is a marginalized, forgotten part of the city," Rev. Martina replied. "It's one thing to talk about a broken system. Now you have gotten to see one up close."

"I feel like this experience is already shattering some of my beliefs, but at the same time it is expanding my frame of reference."

Rev. Martina picked up on Bruce's comment. "What is being shattered?"

"I have always believed that everyone was working for and enjoying a common good, but up until now I never did enough investigation to see if that was really the case. I just assumed that everybody else was getting along as well as I was. I suppose on some level I knew that wasn't true, but before coming here I was able to avoid finding out otherwise."

Rev. Martina pressed Bruce to reflect more. "Are there other things that, to use your word, are being shattered?"

"Well, yeah. Now I am wondering what else I have missed? What other gaps in my experience and understanding do I need to become aware of and explore?"

"Do any come to mind right now?"

"Definitely more about systemic racism and white privilege. I'm sure there are cultural and political gaps. Who knows what else? I guess I don't know what I don't know."

"And what is being expanded?"

"Everything. I feel like I'm drinking from a fire hydrant. I want to experience as much diversity as I can. Even if I never serve in a comparable setting—or perhaps because I may never serve in a comparable setting—I need this experience. I am becoming aware of how undeveloped my understanding of both the gospel and the human condition is. I also think my idea of ministry is being shattered."

"How so?"

"The ministers I have known were nice people who presided over things and were fairly well taken care of by the congregation. In a way, I think a congregation can buy its minister's silence about some of the injustices in our communities. I want to be supported, but not silenced."

Rev. Martina had asked exactly the right question. "What have you learned about yourself from walking our neighborhood?" An African proverb reminds us that it takes a village to raise a child. Likewise, it takes a village to broaden the perspectives and deepen the understanding of those preparing for ministry. Engaging diversity—meeting people, going into new settings, and encountering new circumstances—makes us more aware of our default experiences, which we almost certainly have made normative. This newfound awareness hopefully moves us to interact more broadly. While our ministry may bless the people we encounter, it should also change us such that our understanding becomes more complete. The richness of the diversity will bless our lives.

Billye and the Neighborhood in Transition

Billye became the student pastor at Dove of Peace Church after the congregation determined it could no longer financially support a full-time minister. Years ago, prior to the mid-twentieth century, all the members of Dove of Peace lived within walking distance of the church. The neighborhood, which is located between a resurging downtown area and some very popular suburbs, was self-supporting then, and travel was more limited. As the years passed, the neighborhood changed. Many people moved to distant suburbs, yet continued on as members of the Dove of Peace congregation. The large homes that had been built at the turn of the twentieth century were subdivided into small apartments. The neighborhood became racially, ethnically, and socioeconomically diverse in a way that it had never been before. The members of Dove of Peace showed little interest in the changing neighborhood around the church and even less interest in thinking about how the congregation might relate to their new neighbors. As a result, none of the newer residents have participated in the worship and ministry activities at Dove of Peace. This often happens when most of a congregation's membership lives in areas away from the church's neighborhood.

Dove of Peace was embroiled in conflict when Billye arrived. The decline of membership and resulting financial losses necessitated changes. But most members of the congregation—even those who voted for the change to a part-time minister—resented and resisted those changes. Some blamed the loss of congregational strength on recent pastors. Others said that the congregation would not be in this mess if the church had followed through on its tentative plans, two decades earlier, to relocate to the suburbs. And nearly everyone agreed that what had become of the area around the church, which was the neighborhood where many of the church members had grown up, was a disgrace. The losses had mounted at Dove of Peace—loss of people, resources, influence, way of life, and more. Grief had gripped the congregation. People wanted things to be like they once were. Instead, they were a part of an aging, struggling congregation that was housed in a deteriorating building. Most members of the congregation did not know any of the church's neighbors, and even worse they had little interest in getting to know them.

The congregation's anger and sorrow were evident, and they played it out in unseemly ways. Billye's maturity helped her not to take criticisms and attacks personally. But her first year there was very difficult. She spent a lot of time listening to people in one-on-one and group settings. In addition to the anxiety and grief, she noticed another common thread. Almost without exception, people spoke of the positive difference Dove of Peace had made in that neighborhood over the years. The church had served as something akin to a community center for that area of town. People from all over the city had been in Dove of Peace's building for various meetings and events over the years, but in the midst of undeniable decline the members of the congregation now seemed all alone. They had turned inward as they poured their energy and resources into propping up the organizational machinery of the congregation.

Billye decided to try something. She asked her church board members if they would be willing to have the next board meeting on the front lawn of the church. Some protested and some gladly agreed, but most simply were bewildered: they wondered why they were being asked to do such a thing, and what possible good could come from it. The meeting on the front lawn started the usual way—a prayer, a review of the minutes, discussion of the financial report—but the meeting lost its focus as those in attendance became increasingly distracted by what was going on around them. People began making comments that were completely unrelated to the agenda item under consideration.

"I never knew this was such a busy street during the week," said one woman. "A lot of people drive past our church every day."

"I never realized how many people visit the city park across the street," said another, surprised at how many people walked and rode bicycles in the neighborhood.

A third person, a man who had lived in a larger city during his professional career and only recently had retired to his hometown, noted that this was a much more interesting area of town than he ever imagined. "Who knew this area was so diverse and eclectic?"

It was an eye-opening experience. Demographic studies had not made this kind of impression on them. Ridiculously long meetings had not led to discoveries of this kind. Their preconceived notions had gotten in the way of seeing the area as it really was; but on the night when the Dove of Peace church board and Pastor Billye met on the front lawn what they saw gave them pause. It was not a magical realignment in the relationship between the church and the neighborhood, but it was a liminal moment when the neighborhood seemed to be suspended, if for but a brief but sufficient time, between what it had been and what it was becoming. Thanks to Billye's urging that they meet on the front lawn, people were present to that moment.

Just as the leaders at Dove of Peace awakened to new conversations and possibilities of what it meant to be church in that particular time and place, your search for pastoral voice involves making yourself available and present to what is going on around you. On occasion, those encounters will be joyful and fulfilling, and they will remind you what energizes you for ministry. On other occasions, you will encounter tense conflict, contemplate pastoral risks, and live among people who carry some of grief's heaviest burdens. Whatever the situation, whatever the time or place, you are pressed to consider how each aspect of the context will inform and shape your ministry. These many particularities provide you with reference points as you live within that context and live more fully into your calling.

And so you will ask questions like these: What will be my priorities in ministry? In what ways is helping the congregation find its voice also helping me discover my own pastoral identity? What am I not seeing that would deepen my understanding and clarify my focus for ministry if I were able to bring it into clearer view? To what extent am I allowing others to obstruct or distort my field of vision, and how is that blocking my journey to voice?

CULTIVATING VOICE: STAYING UNTIL YOU LEAVE

Toward the end of commissioning the twelve to "proclaim the good news, cure the sick, raise the dead, cleanse the lepers and cast out demons,"[13] Jesus counsels the disciples on leaving and staying. In regard to leaving, Jesus says, "If anyone will not welcome you or listen to your words, shake off the dust from your feet as you leave that house or town."[14] The time comes at some point for us to leave where we are ministering. However, these days the counsel to "shake the dust off your feet" often gets reworked into a preemptive strike of revenge: Ours is a culture where people's suspicions of each other run high. In many social circles, little excuse is needed for members to distance themselves from other people, and then form rigid closed-loop communities that strive to protect what they perceive to be the truth. In so doing, members form a group that disparages the social positions of other peoples and ignores any economic and religious common ground they share with the outside world.

Jesus also offers a word about staying in a place. "Whatever town or village you enter," he says, "stay there until you leave."[15] Apparently our best chance of curing the sick and raising the dead comes when we are willing to commit to a life of living together. It is no coincidence that some of the most effective times in ministry come when a congregation and a pastor have been together for at least seven or eight years. But most congregations and pastors never experience that golden time because the average relationship between congregation and minister is less than four years.

13. Matt 10:8.
14. Matt 10:14.
15. Matt 10:11.

Stay until you leave. It sounds logically impossible to do otherwise! But some people, unable or unwilling to fully commit, live with one foot out the door of their current location, ministry, or relationship. If we are honest with ourselves, we might remember times when we appeared to be in a place fully but actually had already left it. You might think of that job you held for nearly a decade, but the fact is that you were spending most of the last three years there looking for another job and your mind may have left even a couple of years before that. Or you might think of the seventeen year relationship, but remember that you began checking out after about twelve years and were emotionally absent the last three, even though by all physical appearances you had stayed. You might think of the last church you were a part of, but then remember the lack of enthusiasm and connection you offered during much of that time.

It may feel easier in the short run for us to leave a place rather than to stay, to attempt to recycle ourselves elsewhere rather than to go deeper where we are. But the cultivation of pastoral voice occurs when we remain thoughtfully and honestly present with a group of people over time. Being a pastor is immensely interesting work, but only if we have engaged that work with our imagination, deeply and faithfully. To remain open to the possibilities of ministry we need to sustain our attention and energy through a whole range of seasons and circumstances. Otherwise, the distractions and frustrations of the work will build up to the point that we stay in one sense, but in truth have already left.

The old joke about ministers is this: We move every time we run out of sermons. Many of us move from home, job, relationship, church, or neighborhood at the first sign of conflict, frustration, or lack of appreciation. This, unfortunately, is because greener pastures only materialize when we go deeper with our commitment and practice of presence in a place. Being present for the long-term means being called upon to contribute to the well-being of a place and not just to take from it; it means we must forgive people who will likely hurt us again; it means we must ask for forgiveness for our missteps and mistakes; it means we must recognize the sacred among mundane circumstances; and it means we must actually believe in what we are doing even when the results are less than spectacular. Like any lasting relationship, the best negotiated agreement at the outset is only as good as the numerous renegotiations that occur.

Many field education internships are so brief—sometimes lasting only a semester or two—that student pastors who invest themselves in the learning of the context can feel that they are wasting their time. But what makes these students think life will be any different after they complete seminary? Pastors who have not worked at learning a place usually cannot generate enough genuine interest in any one place to stay beyond a few years. Jesus' words speak to that concern. Wherever we are and for however long we are there—whether that is nine months or nine years—we are encouraged to stay until we leave.

It is to your advantage to remain in a field education placement for a second or even third year in order to experience the cycles of congregational life and to go more deeply into relationships in that church. Not only does this amount of time allow you to develop new clarity, reflections, and interpretations about your context, it also provides you a chance for your love to gradually respond to the place as it really is. In doing so, we can authentically live our lives as part of that place. Herring describes this as "living uncontrived moments."[16] "Inspiration doesn't descend like a lightning bolt from the gods," she says. "Inspiration comes instead from a steady breath, a solid foundation, and a commitment to the process."[17] So it is with ministers and pastoral voice. We must show up day after day, bringing who we are to the steady, consistent engagement of ministry.

And yet, real challenges exist to staying until we leave. For example, our technological culture provides unprecedented access to information. With five clicks of the mouse and in a matter of two or three minutes we can read material that not long ago would have taken six months of library research and extensive travel to obtain. As helpful as this kind of access can be, it can also divert our attention from what is right in front of our eyes. Another distraction surfaces from the minister's own boredom. A minister might blame any feelings of boredom on a complacent congregation or a lifeless town—and there are a few of both out there—but more often than not the boredom lies within the restlessness of the minister's life.

Still another challenge to staying until we leave grows out of the ability—and in some cases, the need—for many of us to relocate relatively easily and frequently. In some cases, new members of a community contribute to the life of the place, but just as often they exploit the community for their own benefit without giving much back. Related to this issue, out of necessity many Americans live different parts of their lives in different

16. Herring, *Writing Begins with the Breath*, 10.
17. Ibid., 13.

communities. They may work in one community, attend church in another, shop in a third, and send their kids to school in a fourth. This lifestyle represents a significant challenge for congregations that are trying to discern their calling and the extent of their programming and mission. Overcoming this obstacle requires that a pastor envision himself or herself as being an integral part of a stable community and, in so doing, lead a congregation to entertain the same vision. Pastoral voice arises from loving a place, and loving a place involves being present to it, regardless of how much we may have already learned about it, how often we have been hurt by it, or how frustrated we are with its limitations.

The spirit with which we enter our ministry sites, whether it is during field education while in seminary or with the congregations we serve after seminary, determines in large measure the degree to which we appreciate our context and thrive in it. Reflecting on the writings of Wendell Berry, Kyle Childress says that a pastor who is considering a new church might be compared to a farmer looking over a piece of land for possible purchase.[18] Berry writes:

> When one buys the farm and moves there to live, something different begins. Thoughts begin to be translated into acts. . . . It invariably turns out, I think, that one's first vision of one's place was to some extent an imposition on it. But if one's sight is clear and one stays on and works well, one's love gradually responds to the place as it really is, and one's vision gradually imagines possibilities that are really in it. . . . It is the properly humbled mind in its proper place that sees truly, because—to give only one reason—it sees details."[19]

As Berry so eloquently notes, humility is at the heart of coming to know and love a place. If we chose not to adopt the humbled mind that Berry speaks of, we likely will continue to see a place as we want to see it. We will not appreciate the life a place had before we arrived, and we likely will impose on it our prejudices and assumptions. In doing so, we will miss recognizing what matters to the people of that place, the rhythms and seasons that shape its life, and the significance of its stories and rituals. The result is that we prove the wisdom of the desert monks: If

18. Childress, "Good Work," 28–33.

19. Berry, *Standing by Words*, 70.

we settle in a place and do not bring forth the fruit of that place, the place itself casts us out.[20]

A properly humbled spirit is a vulnerable spirit, one that is at ease with not knowing and can remain open to the new and different. SCUPE[21] is an experiential educational approach to learning and loving urban ministry. It is based in Chicago and draws students from seminaries around the country. I once heard Dave Frenchak, the founding president of SCUPE, describe the program as one that creates opportunities that allow "the city to touch the heart and the heart to reach out to the city." That phrase beautifully captures the mutuality of every contextual education experience. We enter ministry sites first to be touched by that town or city, and then we give ourselves in return. That vulnerability fosters the discovery and sustains the attentiveness a minister needs to stay in a place until he or she leaves.

A flourishing pastoral imagination involves a thorough understanding of and engagement with what life is like in the community where the church is located. Pastoral voice is impoverished without a vigorous and resilient connection to context. This does not mean that we so completely identify with every aspect of a context that we lose our identity and our ability to speak to its opportunities and challenges with the good news of the gospel. Rather, it means we have such a grasp of the context that we can interpret the ways that congregation and context shape each other and, as a result, we can articulate the congregation's emerging vocation. When you understand where you are, your pastoral voice will embody appreciation, wisdom, and vision. Without those things, your pastoral work will always be in search of a place to take root and grow.

20. Quoted in Norris, *Dakota*, 182. Original source unknown.

21. SCUPE is an acronym that stands for Seminary Consortium for Urban Pastoral Education. For more information, see www.scupe.com.

3

Connecting with the Greater Faith Story

The God one confesses fashions the ministry one practices.[1]

—VICTOR HUNTER

A LIFE-GIVING STORY

IN HIS BOOK *BECOMING a New Church*, Malcolm Warford recalls a conversation he had with a member in the first congregation where he served as pastor. The person said to him, "Basically, what we want to know is what you believe, whether it makes any difference in your life, and how we can learn some things about God and our own lives in watching you." Years later Warford reflected on that exchange by saying, "I have lived in the wonder and terror of those words ever since."[2]

Finding pastoral voice requires that you discover what matters to you as a person of faith. You must then demonstrate what bearing those discoveries, and your commitments to them, have on your life and ministry. Congregations engage in all manner of casual conversation. Some of those conversations carry weight in ways you may not expect. For example, when a church committee interviews you in an effort to discover if you might make a good fit as their pastor that committee may focus

1. Hunter, *Desert Hearts and Healing Fountains*, 55.

2. Warford, *Becoming a New Church*, 110.

on topics that seem somewhat pedestrian to you. Afterward, you may think nothing of those topics. But know that if you get the job, sooner or later members of that committee and the congregation will want to know what those seemingly mundane topics actually mean to you. They will form initial impressions of your pastoral voice through formal moments of preaching and teaching. They will supplement those impressions by observing you in your pastoral roles, which will be in diverse settings and on a variety of occasions. And then, in less formal, more intimate moments, the people in your congregation will listen for your understanding of what it means to be Christian, and they will watch how your understanding informs and shapes you as a person and a minister. Ministry is a crucible of wonder and terror for all who take seriously a call to lead and serve among the people of God. This is another way in which the experiences of field education create an environment in which you can begin to find and claim your pastoral voice. In this way, your field education is a crucible that causes you to think more clearly, compellingly, and practically about your theology.

The Rev. Jerry Falwell gave me a wonderful gift. I don't think it was the gift he intended to give me, and I am sure this gift did not specifically have me in mind, but it remains a gift to this day.

Falwell was a fundamentalist Baptist minister who founded a congregation and, later, a college in Lynchburg, Virginia. His organization, the Moral Majority, melded together a narrow interpretation of Scripture, a slanted view of American history, an intensely conservative social agenda, and significant financial resources to influence American politics—everything from precinct captain elections to the 1980 presidential campaign. I became familiar with Falwell when college friends and I, perhaps with less than noble reasons, would watch his *Old Time Gospel Hour* on cable television.

At that point in my life, I could not articulate my faith in a very coherent or compelling way. But I was sure of one thing: When Falwell taught and preached, he did not speak for me. Little of what he said resonated with me, and much of what he said directly contradicted the gospel that was regularly taught and embodied in my home congregation. I was startled by the difference between the two experiences, both in content and tone.

For example, I grew up hearing about a God whose watchful eye upon us was an expression of divine care and concern; but the watchfulness of

Falwell's God seemed to be more about surveillance and reprimand. We spoke and sang often in our church of the good news that we are never outside of God's love; but on the *Old Time Gospel Hour* our place in the family of God felt tenuous and under continuous review.

I saw how the different ways of speaking of and experiencing God led to a divergence on other matters of faith. In the tradition of my home congregation, ambiguity was acknowledged as a reality and the exploration of faith was encouraged at every turn. That was not the impression that emanated from Falwell's Thomas Road Baptist Church, where it appeared that ambiguity was a sign of weak faith. To guard against that slippery slope, Falwell's ministry provided answers and discouraged curiosity.

While, at my home congregation, we attempted to follow in the way of Jesus of Nazareth and sought the Bible's guidance; we also interacted with other religious traditions and listened prayerfully to nonreligious voices that could expand and enhance our faith. On the other hand, no one incurred the wrath of Falwell more than the secular humanists in our midst who, in his estimation, were craftily leading church and country alike down a path of destruction. Falwell spoke frequently about the Bible containing all the truth needed to live a Godly life, but some passages seemed to be more true than others. Those particular passages seemed to function as a filter through which all other parts of the Bible had to pass. Even verses that dripped with the sweetness of God's unceasing mercy were reinterpreted by Falwell's ministry as being only occasionally applicable.

Perhaps most striking of all was how, in Falwell's mind, the world was divided between good and evil. For a man who proclaimed that God was in control, Falwell seemed overly concerned that evil had a growing foothold that threatened the souls of individuals and the future of the world. In our church, where politeness reigned supreme and transgressions were named privately and even then in the most hushed of tones, sin was rarely mentioned in public worship, much less confessed. Despite some noticeable shortcomings, the members of my home congregation generally experienced the world on beautiful and hopeful terms. We recognized some of our human limitations, but for the most part we lived with God's pronouncement of the goodness of creation, and the love of God's voice echoed in our ears and reverberated in our being.

The *Old Time Gospel Hour* contained a gift for me, plain and simple, and I still benefit from that gift all these years later. The gift was not that I had been given permission to believe that the whole truth of the Christian faith was lodged with our church, or that the realm of God was more evident at our church than at his. Rather, the gift was that of clarification, wrapped in different voices from within the Christian family. While some of what Falwell taught was horrifying, most all of his teachings provided something against which to define and elucidate, however provisionally, my own understanding of the Christian faith. We did not do much of that in the church where I grew up. Much of our faith was defined by civic commitments to respectability, honesty, hard work, loyalty, optimism, and status quo. We occasionally allowed Jesus to critique the unintended consequences of those commitments, but not as often as we should have.

So, in no small way, a person who represented radically different and even hostile views on important matters became an important teacher to me. At this point, I am still more closely aligned with the tradition of my home congregation than with Falwell's teaching, but he pushed me to think about certain questions that otherwise I might not have entertained until much later. These questions were integral to the discovery of my pastoral voice: How would I articulate the authority of Scripture while seeking the counsel of other voices, both religious and nonreligious? If there are many paths to God and many experiences of God, what does it mean to say that Jesus is Lord and Savior? Why did our church never speak of evil, even though evidence of brokenness and destruction was all around us? What messages of exclusion did our obviously well-heeled, well-connected congregation send to people in our town who were from different social circles, economic classes, races, and backgrounds? And even if people like me found Falwell's convictions appallingly rigid and narrow, was our shortsightedness just as apparent yet simply centered in a different set of rigidly held convictions?

So it was not the case that I rejected Falwell's teaching so that I could keep embracing, without reconsideration, what I already believed. Rather, Falwell provided me with a clarifying challenge to discover what I understood about the Christian faith and, unwittingly, sent me on a journey of interrogation and reflection toward a deeper understanding and experience of faith.

Later, as I began to discern a call to ministry, I had a similar experience in my local area churches. It was not unusual at that time for local congregations to invite people who were considering ministry to be guest preachers, regardless of denominational or theological differences. Some of those settings were similar to my home church, but others introduced me to screaming from the pulpit, high-pressure invitations, blood hymns, and the cunning ways of the Devil. I quickly discovered that the television had provided me with an excellent buffer when I watched Falwell. But in these area congregations I was not only in the thick of the action all around me, I could not turn it off. Some of what I experienced was edifying, some of it was manipulative and injurious. Participating in the worship of those congregations provided me with points of clarification about the Christian faith in general, the practices of the church itself, and some truths about my own pastoral voice.

Still later, through my seminary studies, I engaged the church's story and theology in much greater breadth and depth. The same will occur for you, if it has not already. When you are a student serving a congregation, you get to experience that history and thought up close. All around you will be expressions of belief, practices that convey aspects of the tradition, and ongoing conversations about what constitutes a lively Christian identity and witness in your particular setting. As a student minister, you are wonderfully positioned to grasp and claim the greater story of which you are a part. That is good news, not just for the sake of your own spirituality and discipleship, but also because you are preparing to be a key teacher and interpreter of the faith in a congregation. Through a myriad of experiences you are attempting to cultivate a pastoral voice that nurtures a particular kind of community and calls that community, as followers of Jesus, to embody a vital identity and witness. This chapter, then, seeks to cultivate your pastoral voice in relation to those beliefs and practices.

THEOLOGICAL PREPARATION SHAPES DAILY MINISTRY

A masters of divinity degree does not qualify a person for many professional paths. It does, however, prepare one to be a resident theologian with a local community of faith. And yet, many seminary graduates seem to back away from this aspect of the ministry and instead spend inordinate amounts of time attempting to administer programs, manage budgets, counsel parishioners, perform building maintenance, and oversee an office and staff. Many pastors complain about how unfulfilling these aspects of ministry are, yet these same pastors do not seem eager to reclaim the role of teacher with any vigor or appreciation. This is a curious phenomenon because this teaching role is what drew many pastors to consider ministry in the first place. This is not to say pastors should not be involved in the business and administrative aspects of ministry, rather I mean to call attention to what should be the primary pastoral role, which is teaching and interpreting the faith in every pastoral task, activity, and setting.

Pastors are not the only ones responsible for interpreting the Christian story to the congregation, but this work lies at the heart of the pastoral vocation. And yet, teaching and interpreting the faith is a feature of pastoral voice that is sorely neglected. For example, individuals and congregations live daily with competing stories that shape their thoughts and commitments. One story may emphasize radical individualism while another urges the priority be placed on a community. Or, one story may highlight a worldview thoroughly shaped by America's power and might, while a story about widespread hunger and poverty in the world may evoke an entirely different worldview. We live among the many competing stories of retailers, politicians, sports teams, and social agendas. The viewpoints and agendas of each of these entities clamor for our attention and allegiance. People struggle to determine what storyline should and will receive their devotion as people of faith. In the church's history, various stories have competed for prominence and support and that competition continues to the present day, whether we are talking about the style of worship, proper belief, or correct stands on moral issues. As pastor, your role is to help individuals and congregations find their place in a greater story, one that gives them life and hope, one that puts all the hollow and death-dealing stories into proper perspective. The quality of your theological clarity and depth are essential in successfully fulfilling this role.

Some seminaries require that students accept certain creeds or other explicit statements as being a truthful and comprehensive articulation of the Christian faith. At other seminaries, the prevailing theology and ethos will not be stated so openly, but students can quickly accumulate enough clues to discover the school's dominant stances and commitments. The extent to which students must actually agree with the guiding assumptions of their school is up for debate. Some students will accept their school's theology uncritically; others will reject some or all of it, also uncritically. Whether you agree or disagree with the teachings of your school, the more pressing question is this: What is the biblical and theological basis of your assent or divergence?

Frequently, seminaries ask students to write their own credos. If you have already written one, this is a good time to review it, note what has changed, if anything, and then revise your credo to reflect any new or different understanding of the Christian faith. If you have not written a credo yet, the following questions from a *A Faith of Your Own* provide a good starting point for doing so.[3]

1. I believe that we formulate our interpretations of Christian faith by drawing on the following resources_____.

2. I believe in a God who is _____.

3. I believe that Jesus Christ is _____.

4. I believe that the Holy Spirit is _____.

5. I believe in the Trinity as _____ (if you believe in the concept of Trinity).

6. I believe that God's ultimate purposes are _____.

7. I believe that the church is _____ (nature and purpose of the church).

8. I believe that evil is _____.

9. I believe that the relationship of the church to other religions is _____.

It seems to me that belief is downplayed these days in our larger culture. Some people say that it does not matter at all what we believe. But when people, for instance, fly airplanes into buildings in the name of God, or demean other human beings with the words of Scripture, or use a twisted eschatological slant as rationale for exploiting creation, we are presented with a startling reminder that religious belief can be used for destructive forces. Then we have to rethink whether beliefs matter.

Because beliefs matter, you must reflect upon what you believe and how you believe it. What have been the clarifying sources and moments in your faith journey? How has your understanding of God changed through the years? How do you articulate the authority of Scripture? What do you believe that God desires for the world and how have you come to hold that view?

3. Allen, *A Faith of Your Own*, 130–31.

Whatever theological twists and turns you have encountered thus far, know that more are ahead. Seminary will provide you with many opportunities to think prayerfully and practically about your theological positions. After seminary, rigorous preparation to teach the faith will offer you further occasions through which to clarify and deepen your understanding.

One seasoned pastor preached a sermon series entitled "This I Believe," patterned after the National Public Radio series by the same name. This pastor reported that preparing and preaching that sermon series represented important and exciting chapters in an unfolding journey of his faith and ministry. Other opportunities will provide you with similar experiences. In small group settings you may be identified as the leader or facilitator, and, as a result of that experience, you may find yourself rethinking what you know, and in this way learn from the members of the group. Some of the books you will read, or reread, after seminary will influence your thinking and rejuvenate your ministry in substantial ways. You may do some of this reading simply out of personal interest, but through engaging in interesting ideas and writers you will support the teaching and interpreting that you do for a community of faith.

WHERE THE CHRISTIAN STORY COMES TO LIFE

In field education, the Christian story is found at every turn. We cannot escape it. And yet, even with its signs and symbols everywhere, we do not always notice it or grasp its implications.

This section offers three detailed illustrations of experiencing a worship service and shorter descriptions of a church board meeting and a spiritual life small group. These illustrations are designed to show you some of the ways that you will likely encounter the Christian story in your field education experience. Various aspects of each scenario will be introduced, which are then followed by questions that are designed to help you see more clearly the theological underpinnings of your congregation's identity, commitments, and practices. Each question will yield clues on its own—for example, the mode of baptism might signal certain beliefs and practices—but the greater value is when several of these responses are taken together and begin to form a more complete picture. It likely will be a complex picture and, at places, even a contradictory one, but those instances of comparison and contrast will offer clarification for you.

In preparation, you should consider the following questions. They are intended to prompt you to reflect in two areas: faith and practice; and your connections to the Christian story.

1. Within what stream of Christian faith and practice can your congregation be found? What do you see and hear that causes you to identify your congregation with that particular stream? And to what extent does your congregation embrace, modify, or reject that identity?

2. From what you are seeing and hearing in your congregation, what are you learning about your own connection to the Christian story? Is this a theological home for you or a foreign land where many things do not resonate? What from these encounters with the Christian story do you want and need to know more about in order to foster your pastoral voice?

The first illustration has to do with worship. Let us suppose that your congregation has a single worship service on Sunday morning, and that you are arriving at the church in advance of that worship service. Before you even enter the building, what clues exist on the outside of the church building that reveal the particular faith story of your congregation?

- Does the sign outside the church reveal anything about how the congregation sees itself in relation to the Christian story?

- Is there anything theological in the name of the congregation that warrants further investigation? For example, it seems likely that a congregation named "Community of Reconciliation" is paying more attention to different theological impulses than does a congregation whose church is named "Word of Life Lutheran Church."

- Is there a denominational affiliation listed on the sign and, if so, what might that reveal about your congregation's commitments and practices? For example, a sign that indicates an affiliation with the Assemblies of God suggests something different from a church that displays an affiliation with the Unitarian Universalists. The deeper questions, however, have to do with how your congregation views those differences. In what ways does your congregation value and play down the relationship it has with other denominations?

After you note the church sign and any other hints outside the building about what being a Christian church means to this congregation, you continue your discovery by going inside.

- What do you see in the sanctuary and, based on how the space is organized, what at first glance do you think is important to the congregation?
- What symbols are present and what do you suppose they represent, if anything?
- At the front of the sanctuary, do you see a chancel or a stage?
- Do you see an altar or a communion table at the center?
- Is the pulpit also at the center or is it positioned to either the right or left?
- Is the place for baptism a font or baptistery?
- What can you discern about the congregation's worship after briefly flipping through the hymnal and considering its organization?
- Are there Bibles available in the pews? What translation?
- Do flags adorn the front of the sanctuary and, if so, which ones and what do they communicate?
- Were you given a printed order of worship on the way into the sanctuary? If so, what clues can be found in it about how the congregation understands God and practices the faith? And if there is no printed order of worship, does that reveal anything in particular about the congregation's theology or practical preferences?

Now let us assume that you have taken a seat and the service is about to start. As with the earlier questions, the following questions are intended to provoke you. Many of them suggest a wide continuum of answers on which you can locate your theological understanding and that of the congregation.

- How does the service begin and who do you see as worship begins? The pastor? Is the pastor male or female? Is there more than one pastor? Is the pastor dressed in a polo shirt, or business attire, or in a robe with a stole? Who else participates in the leadership of worship? Are both males and females included in those roles?

- Is it clear what is expected of the worshippers during the service?

- What is conveyed about God, Jesus, humans, and the church by the choice of hymns and songs? A service that starts with "Immortal, Invisible, God Only Wise" likely will take on a different tone than one that begins with "Lord, I Lift Your Name on High."

- Is a creed or an affirmation of faith recited? What appears to be happening in that moment? Is it a sign of unanimous doctrinal agreement, or an expression of connection to an earlier Christian community, or a perfunctory statement of beliefs said by people who have not thought much about what they are saying?

- Is there a single Scripture reading or are there several? How does the Scripture tie into the rest of the service? What introduction is given to the reading? In thinking about how this congregation understands the authority of Scripture, would you say that the reading is "the word of the Lord" or "some musings about God from the ancient middle-eastern world"?

- Does the service include preaching? If so, how does the preaching relate to the Scriptures, creeds, and hymns in the service?

- Does the service include the sacred meal? If the sacred meal is not offered on this particular day, does worship ever include the Lord's Supper? If the Supper is included, what is it called? Eucharist? Communion? The Lord's Supper? Sacred meal? Do clergy, laypersons, or some combination of the two preside at the table? What clues can you gather about the church from the invitation to the table: Who is and who is not welcome to participate? What theological content can be heard in the prayers? Is this meal a feast of joy for those gathered, or a foretaste of the heavenly banquet, or the sobering reminder of a substitutionary sacrifice made by Jesus? Is the sacred meal made of bread and wine, or is it the body and blood of Jesus?

- At some point of the service, either after the sermon or at the end, is there an invitation extended to those in the congregation who wish to make a public confession of faith? What is asked of those who respond to that invitation? And if no invitation is offered, what ways are provided for the congregation to respond to having heard and witnessed the gospel?

- At the close of worship, what is the nature of the benediction? Does it offer a blessing on individuals, or a charge to Christian living, or both? Do people simply leave church, or are they sent?

The second illustration has to do with meeting your congregation's governing board. Various traditions and congregations use different names for this group, but essentially we are talking about that group of leaders who are charged with oversight for staff, finances, buildings and property, and the well-being and witness of the congregation. Other boards, councils, or groups may take direct responsibility for the details of some of these matters, but final approval typically rests with a governing board of some type that makes decisions on behalf of the congregation. Imagine that you are observing that meeting as a way to help you think more about how the Christian story influences the week-to-week life of your congregation.

- Who is present at the meeting? What other roles do these people play in the congregation? Is the meeting presided over by a clergy person or a layperson? If the pastor does not preside, what is the pastor's role in the meeting?

- Are any explicitly theological matters discussed? For example, the board might be asked to support an evangelistic effort to new residents in the area, or a ministry for nearby homeless people, or a restructuring of Sunday school.

- On the other hand, what implicit theological assumptions and issues are present yet unaddressed in the discussions? Is the congregation "going on faith" in some regard and, if so, what does that seem to mean to them?

- How are decisions made during the meeting? By following Robert's Rules of Order? By prayerful discernment? By vote or consensus? By some combination of all of these?

- Are there decisions that directly affect the congregation that the congregation does not have the power to make? For example, is the pastor appointed to the congregation by a bishop? Is the congregation's property and building owned by the denomination?

- What is conveyed about the well-being of the congregation and its belief about God in the way it goes about its business? Is there hopefulness and energy? Anxiety and timidity? Division and resentment? Grief and fatigue?

- To what extent does the congregation's calling inform matters being discussed and decisions being made?

- What is the collective spirituality of this group; and what difference does it make in what matters the group takes up and how they address them?[4]

- Is there any sign that the congregation sees itself as adventurously participating in the purposes of God in the world? Or does the congregation exist only for its own fellowship? Does the congregation act for the sake of a flourishing future or does it act against its own best interest?

The third illustration has to do with your participation in the spiritual life of a small group. Imagine that you are sitting with eight to ten other people in someone's living room. The purpose of the group is to help its members cultivate a vibrant spiritual life by way of spending time in prayer together and by encouraging and supporting the personal prayer life of each member. The meeting usually begins with an informal check-in to see how everyone is doing, and then continues with a reading from Scripture and silent and spoken prayer. Most of the time each meeting is spent reflecting on where and how each member has experienced God in his or her life during the week. The meeting provides numerous angles from which to understand how this group understands itself in relationship to the Christian story. These questions should prompt a few of those reflections.

- How is God addressed by the group's participants? Is God as Father the predominant image? Are other biblical images and contemporary metaphors used?

- Do people pray also to Jesus or the Spirit? And if they pray in Jesus' name, what are they conveying about Jesus when they do so?

- How would this group describe what it means to have a vibrant spiritual life?

---

4. For examples of these types, see Israel Galindo, *The Hidden Lives of Congregation*.

- What can you surmise about the theological leanings of this group based on the Scriptures that are chosen and what members say about them?

- How do the people in this group understand their relationship to the rest of the congregation, its denominational family, the wider community?

- In addition to Scripture, does the group's discussion of the spiritual life include reflecting on the lives of other Christians, such as St. Francis of Assisi, Teresa of Avila, Thomas Merton, or Julian of Norwich?

- Are nonbiblical resources used in this group and, if so, what do they convey about God and the Christian faith?

- Do the participants only speak of God working in their lives when they have experienced good fortune, or do they also speak of a God who challenges and calls them beyond themselves?

- What do the participants identify as being the most persistent obstacles to a vibrant spiritual life? Lack of time? The devil? Affluence? And what support does the group provide for dealing with those obstacles?

- Does God seem to be more transcendent than immanent, or vice versa?

- Do people speak openly about times when it felt like God was absent from their lives and the life of the world?

Forming a Theological Picture

You will not answer all of these questions from participating in one worship service, or one board meeting, or one spiritual life group. Instead, you will circle back to these congregational moments again and again with these and other questions to look for clues and piece together a picture, so that over time you can come to an informed idea of how your congregation relates to the Christian story. By way of these experiences and reflections, you may find that your theology and practice to be inconstant and erratic. Do not be discouraged; rather think of this as a call for you to sort out your own beliefs within the greater faith story. As seasons of intentional reflection pass by, you will become increasingly aware of your theological assumptions and perspectives and become significantly more nimble in talking about them. As Kathleen Cahalan writes, "For theology to become second nature for ministers they need to practice drawing upon doctrines, narratives, symbols, and paradigms that constitute the Christian tradition. As they become more adept and confident, they also become more creative and imaginative. But such facility takes time and practice."[5]

You will understand and find your theological and ecclesial home by continuing to pay attention to what regularly and episodically occurs in the congregation you are serving. In some cases, you will receive confirmation that the theological understanding and commitments of a particular congregation offers you a place where you can flourish in ministry. In others, the theology and rituals will not resonate with you and you will recognize the need to think further about the family of faith that you will call your own. In the process, your pastoral voice will be enhanced as you explore how your vocational path intersects with various expressions of the Christian story. This is especially the case when thinking about ordination, as follows:

- Are you seeking or not seeking ordination; and what reasons support the decision you have made?

- What does ordination mean to you and to your church?

- Why are you seeking ordination in a particular tradition as opposed to another one? For example, to be ordained a Roman Catholic priest carries a very different meaning as compared with being ordained a Disciples of Christ minister.

- What beliefs, attributes, and priorities in your denominational family do you embrace enthusiastically; and which ones cause you concern and frustration?

- What is your understanding of worship, baptism, preaching, and the Lord's Supper?

- With these and other questions, what do you draw on in the Christian story to support theological positions and pastoral practices?

For as long as you engage in ministry and seek after God, you should reflect on the intimate and tangible ways that the Christian story comes to life. At your best, you will find yourself in a constructive spiral of

---

5. Cahalan, "Introducing Ministry," 111.

reflection and practice, learning and reappraisal. Your understanding will deepen at every turn of that spiral, and so will your pastoral voice.

HOW THE CHRISTIAN STORY GIVES RISE TO PASTORAL VOICE: SOME CASE STUDIES

The following two case studies show how practical and concrete engagement with the Christian story plays out in the life of a congregation and in the development of your pastoral voice.

Juanita and the Liturgical Year

Juanita came to seminary because she had an unrelenting suspicion that her nondenominational megachurch had only allowed her into the foyer of a grand mansion. She told her field education director, "There has to be more to our faith than what I am hearing about at my church. I want to know more of the Christian story, understand how it has unfolded, and find my place in it." A few months later, Juanita began learning more about the Christian story through an internship at St. Mark's United Church of Christ. Worship, in particular, offered her a life-nourishing encounter with God while at the same time raising many questions for her about the church's theology. For example, Juanita noticed that the worship bulletin always referred to a particular Sunday in two ways. In addition to the date from the Gregorian calendar, it also noted the date in terms of the liturgical year. For the date of December 9, 2012, for example, the worship bulletin noted that it was the Second Sunday of Advent. On January 13, 2013, for example, the worship bulletin indicated that it was The Baptism of Christ Sunday. Juanita had read a little about the liturgical year, but she had never participated in its rhythms nor had she known how much theology and church history can be learned from studying its patterns.

When Advent began, Juanita marveled at the idea of spending several weeks prior to Christmas with biblical stories and congregational practices that focused on waiting, longing, and preparing. It gave her pause to imagine people holding on to promise and hope, as described in the early chapters of Isaiah, while experiencing a sense of God's absence and delay. Advent questions bubbled up in her. Is God not always present with us? Does God occasionally step into human history in remarkable ways and, if so, what does it take to prompt God to do that? Who are the people around us now who are experiencing the absence of God, and what good news do we have for them? What place does waiting have in my spiritual life? And when we sing "O come, O come, Emmanuel," are we actually prepared for the disruption that Emmanuel's appearance may bring to our lives?

Before her experiences at St. Mark's, Juanita viewed Christmas Eve as the culmination of a long and peculiar stretch of repulsive commercialism mixed with vague religious trimmings. Now she welcomed the twelve days of Christmas as a time to immerse herself in an incarnational mystery that could not be fully captured in one worship service on a single night. She contemplated how a ruthless king like Herod could be frightened by a baby born on the economic and political margins. She reflected on the humanity and divinity of Jesus, how he is alike and different from the rest of us, and whether he was born as God's chosen or became the Christ as a result of the community's affirmation of his unusual wisdom, courage, and spirituality. The season also sent Juanita searching for how the date for the Christmas celebration was determined so that she may understand why the date is different in some parts of the church.

On the Sundays following Epiphany, stories about Jesus being recognized as God's beloved intersected with Juanita's struggle to sort through the claims that faith traditions make about their paths to God. Are we talking about the same God? What does it mean to claim Jesus as the Christ, and what are the implications for interfaith dialogue from doing so? Is there equal truth in all of these traditions? Are there things Christians can learn, even should learn, as a result of interacting with Jews, Buddhists, Hindus, and Muslims?

Juanita had never attended an Ash Wednesday service before, much less participated in its leadership. Nor had she considered in any systematic way the stories that described Jesus' deliberate journey to Jerusalem and the events of Holy Week that led to his execution. Her experiences with Lenten introspection and self-denial brought to the surface questions that she had not yet considered. How does acknowledging our finiteness as human beings give shape and direction to our lives? What are the purposes of God for my life and for the world? To what extent did Jesus' own actions lead to his death? Other than substitutionary atonement, are there ways that the meaning of Jesus' death is interpreted in the

New Testament and in church tradition? What does it mean for us to take up our crosses, and what might the consequences be for doing so?

On Easter Sunday, Juanita experienced a community of faith that was awash in new life. The hope and joy of the risen Christ seemed to touch every person and every act of worship. Amid the alleluias came unexpected issues. At her former congregation, Easter focused on God raising the physical body of Jesus, but at St. Mark's it was not clear to Juanita whether resurrection had to include the resuscitation of Jesus' body. The pastor described Easter as "the triumph of God"—the good news that corruption, hatred, and death do not have the final word in this life or the next. This truth resonated with Juanita, but she knew that prejudice, suffering, and destruction in the world had not ended that Easter morning. What did it mean, she wondered, to celebrate the triumph of God when so many people and places had not yet experienced the victory?

Pentecost brought more of the same energy and inquiry to Juanita's faith journey. The worship service at St. Mark's celebrated the beginning of the church and the church's charge to be a blessing to its participants and to the world. But Juanita got hung up on the Holy Spirit. She wondered: Is this the same spirit of God that was at work from the beginning, or are we being introduced to a new entity? And if the Holy Spirit is a new character in the story, does the Spirit flow from God or from Jesus? Is the Holy Spirit a manifestation of God? What does it mean to be Trinitarian? And to what extent does the church affirm or deny that the Spirit is poured out on all flesh?

Worship at St. Mark's confirmed Juanita's suspicion that the Christian story is a vast mansion that stands open for inspection. Juanita visited every room she could find. Each new discovery clarified her thinking and connected her to a faith story that was greater than she had previously been able to imagine.

Jody's Rethinking of Sin and Evil

As Jody learned more about church history and thought, she was surprised to learn that some of her deepest faith commitments had been shaped by a rather liberal expression of the Christian tradition. Very few in her Disciples of Christ congregation would have described themselves as being liberal, and nothing in her hometown suggested that liberalism had much of a foothold there. Both the church and the community gave the outward impression of a settled and conservative place that probably looked askance upon much social variation. And yet, key elements of theological liberalism—the critical study of Scripture, wisdom from the broader community, the value of personal experience, the resistance to rigid doctrines, an emphasis on the exemplary nature of Jesus' life, and an optimistic view of human potential—had deeply influenced the thought and practices of her congregation. Looking back, she marveled at how she was able to hold on to that view of humanity in the midst of mounting evidence to the contrary. The first time she heard and participated in a Confession of Sin during worship was in a seminary chapel service. The experience caught her off-guard emotionally. Her faith journey, up to that point, prompted her to celebrate that we humans are made just a little lower than God and are crowned with glory and honor.[6]

When Jody became the student pastor of Calvary Christian Church, she did not have the theological space for the heart-wrenching reality of that congregation's pain. She found herself in a congregational setting that presented her with an ample number of painful experiences, and she began to rethink her prior beliefs. Four years earlier, an elder in that church had been charged with sexually abusing seven children in the congregation and three of his own grandchildren. The man, who was in his sixties when he violated the children, pled guilty and soon began serving a forty-four year prison sentence. The legal side of this horrific event concluded quickly and neatly while the emotional processes in the congregation were just beginning. Several counselors and consultants helped the congregation move through the next couple of years. An interim minister had been a healing presence, but he was not able to stop the exodus of church members who left for other churches or, in many cases, to no church at all. By the time Calvary was ready to think about calling a new pastor, the church did not have finances to support a full-time person. So, Calvary considered other possibilities and, before very long, called Jody to be their first student and first female pastor.

Some healing continued to occur during Jody's three years as pastor at Calvary, but reminders of what had happened persisted. The guilty man had two adult children who continued to participate in the congregation, though they did so to a significantly lesser degree than before. Two of the

6. Ps 8:5.

kids who had been abused and their families also stayed on at Calvary. Close friends of the man in the church tried to come to grips with what had happened and what it revealed about the human condition in general. Through all of this, Jody tried to reconcile her old view of pervasive human goodness with the truths of stunning human failure and pain.

Prior to serving at Calvary, Jody had not grappled with such theological intersections. She understood the world to be a friendly place where good people worked together for a common good. She knew that other church traditions characterized the world as being a fearful and evil place where human beings are incapable of choosing a good path on their own. That had not been her understanding, however, because she had never experienced fear and evil in an immediate and personal way.

Jody began finding her pastoral voice as a result of exploring questions that were raised by the awfulness that had occurred at Calvary. She asked herself, What is the human condition, and what in the Christian story informs it? Are we infinitely good, or totally depraved, or some mixture of promise and peril? What is the story of Adam and Eve in the garden trying to tell us about the freedom of human beings and the limits of human potential? What is Paul trying to say about sin when he describes his own inner conflict?[7] Are sin and evil the same things or does one precede the other?

She pressed the inquiry deeper. How do we speak of God's love and judgment in the midst of this discussion? Are we of infinite value to God despite our stunning finiteness? Was it necessary for Jesus to die in our place in order for us to gain a right relationship with God? Or was the execution of Jesus another example of evil spinning out of control? Does God redeem death-dealing situations in our lives with new life?

In the midst of the brokenness at Calvary, Jody particularly wanted to gain clarity around forgiveness and healing. People at Calvary wanted to forgive, but they found it difficult to do so. They wanted the guilty man to be assured of God's love, but they wanted him to remember also the pain he had caused and the wrongs he had done. Jody had more questions: Do we forgive for others' sake or for our own? Does the community of faith play a role in mediating God's forgiveness? And what does healing mean in a journey that most certainly will involve future loss and betrayal?

7. Rom 7:15.

Jody's gracious presence allowed the congregation at Calvary the space it needed to think about the pain that humans visit upon one another and to see human kindness and resilience in the face of desperate moments. While she would have never wished such tragedy upon a congregation, the chance to be that congregation's pastor changed her life and ministry by causing her to revisit the previously underdeveloped portions of her theology. Her questions about sin and evil led her to numerous other theological and ecclesial concerns that warranted exploration. Jody coupled pastoral sensitivities with insightful preaching and teaching, which then resulted in Calvary thinking more clearly and hopefully about what it means to be a church and to be held always, despite limitations and heartbreaks, in the embrace of God's love. Ministry at Calvary deepened Jody's voice. As a result of Jody's voice, life at Calvary was different.

CULTIVATING VOICE: PERFORMING THEOLOGY

One pastor led a six-week Bible study on economic justice. The group met at its church for the first four weeks and they explored the issue from the perspective of Israelite enslavement in Egypt, the Old Testament prophets, stories and teachings from the life of Jesus, and examples of how the early church dealt with economic justice. On the fifth week, the group met off-site at a rally for fair wages and working conditions for hotel workers in their city. When someone in the group asked the pastor why they were going to that rally, she responded, "What better way to study economic justice than to see the exploitation of the poor up close? We've read in Scripture how that exploitation angers God. Now we are going to hear about it from people in our own community and see what reaction it stirs in us. It's just a continuation of our Bible study."

The final and sixth week of this Bible study class also included a field trip. This time the group traveled to the annual meeting of an interfaith organization that had been working with congregations and elected officials on issues of unemployment, public transportation, education, and crime. Before boarding church vans and driving across town to the meeting, the pastor gave some background to group members. "Tonight people from various faith communities from all over the city will describe what they have been doing in the area of economic justice. You will learn about specific strategies and direct action, what we perceive to be the positive impact of those efforts, and the particular issues we need to focus on next. This is the 'so-what?' of our Bible study. Think about what we discussed during the first four weeks. Now that we have a better idea of what Scripture says, so what? Think about what we heard and observed and felt at last week's rally. Now that we know some of those who carry a disproportionate burden of our economic systems and policies, so what? How does any of this understanding and experience claim our time and energy and gifts? What implications does any of this raise for our lives?"

Theology is performative. As interesting as theological discussions and debates can be, these conversations should lead somewhere. You may have the most beautifully crafted credo in the history of Christianity, but what happens next? What does it look like to perform your credo? For example, if you understand hospitality to be at the heart of the gospel, is hospitality woven through everything you do as a pastor? If you believe that flourishing spirituality depends on continual Bible study and prayer, can those things easily be identified, based on how you spend your time, as a significant priority in your ministry? In short, does your ministry flow from how you understand God, what you believe about Jesus, and how you interpret the purpose of the church; or does your credo express disembodied and compartmentalized views that do not inform the way you actually think, speak, and act?

In his letter to the Philippians, Paul urged that young Christian congregation to perform its theology. Paul had begun the church in Philippi several years before writing this letter, which is an intimate glimpse of a mutually appreciative relationship between Paul and the Christians in Philippi. Paul clearly wrote at a time when that community was experiencing the stress of internal angst and external threats. In prison at the time and unable to go himself, Paul wants to show his concern for the congregation by sending Timothy. When Epaphroditus is well enough to travel, Paul will send him, too, but in the meantime Paul gives the Philippians some instructions by way of letter. After reminding them to have the same mind and the same love that was in Christ Jesus, Paul tells them, "Finally, beloved, whatever is true, whatever is honorable, whatever is just, whatever is pure, whatever is pleasing, whatever is commendable, if there is any excellence and if there is anything worthy of praise, think about these things. Keep on doing the things that you have learned and received and heard and seen in me, and the God of peace will be with you."[8]

"Do these things," Paul says. Perform in your lives, as individuals and as a congregation, what you know to be the gospel of Christ Jesus. Paul describes an experience of God that does not come from arguing someone else down, but comes through practicing those things that are at the heart of the Christian story with the hope that they will become the center of the life of the church and the world. Paul raises several themes and issues in the course of this letter, but then near the end he offers his own "so what?" More than just asking the congregation at Philippi to agree that the way of Jesus Christ brings life and light and love, Paul calls his friends to practice the way of Jesus, to perform it, in their own lives.

Theology that is performative leads to an imaginative discipleship and a daring faithfulness. Such a theology calls forth gifts that animate the worship, learning, fellowship, and witness of a congregation and helps its members actively pursue a more just, loving, peaceful, hopeful life for all of God's people. As Elaine Graham has described it, performative or practical theology is value-directed and value-laden action. Our practice of ministry takes on the values and priorities of the gospel and causes them to come alive in concrete ways. Together, the pastor and congregation intentionally enact their understanding of the gospel in specific ways.[9] This is not a new idea, of course. Paul urged the Philippians to "do these things." Well before Paul, the people of Israel were instructed to "do justice."[10] And yet, the anxiety and reactivity of many pastors and congregations foster an unhealthy togetherness that does not allow much room for the challenge of the gospel. Instead, congregations naturally and quickly gravitate toward what is comfortable and convenient. As a result, discoveries made through contextual study get shelved, pastoral roles devolve into congregational chaplain, and Bible study becomes an interesting but irrelevant and disembodied exercise.

So how do we arrive at a performative theology? Or, to use Paul's words, what does the move from thinking on these things to doing them actually look like?

---

8. Phil 4:8–9.

9. Graham, *Transforming Practice*, 111.

10. Mic 6:8.

The way I approach this with students is to ask them to write a four-part paper that ties the vocation of the church to God's ultimate purposes. In the first part, I ask students to answer the question, "What does God desire for the world?" Christians answer that question in different ways, of course. Some believe that God's desire for the world is for every individual to know and experience personal salvation through Jesus Christ. Others speak of the healing of creation. Some Christians envision world peace being at the heart of God's hope for the world. Still others posit the hope that rich and poor will live together on a level, equally accessible and beneficial economic playing field. Some hold that discerning and preserving the truth of God as it relates to worship or doctrine or right living is the ultimate concern. In the Hebrew Bible, God desires shalom, which is wholeness and well-being based on justice, truth, and peace. Jesus described the hope of shalom as living an abundant life.[11] Many Christians affirm several of these positions, and the distinctions between them have to do with degrees of emphasis.

For the second part of this assignment, I ask students to consider the question, "In light of God's desire for the world, what do you understand the vocation of the church to be?" A few years ago everybody was writing a mission statement—schools, hospitals, corporations, individuals, and yes, congregations. Most congregational mission statements suffer from the need to be approved by a committee or board. The resulting statements were somewhat religious sounding, but they were cast in such vague terms that they really gave no clues about the perspective and hope of the congregation. In most cases, it was not clear that the congregations had contemplated God's ultimate purposes in formulating their mission statements. (Perhaps doing so would have resulted in the mission statement never getting out of committee.)

Let us then forego the trend of creating mission statements in response to this question. A better response begins with posing another question: How would the conversations within a church change if the presence and purposes of God were taken as the starting point for any discussion about the vocation of the church? For example, what if a reply to the understanding of church vocation resulted from prayerful engagement with the call of Mic 6:8 to do justice, love mercy, and walk humbly with your God? Or perhaps such a reply could begin with Luke 4:18–19

11. John 10:10.

and the urging to proclaim good news to the poor, release to the prisoners, and bring recovery of sight to the blind. Still another way to formulate a reply is to ground ministry in what God desires for the world, and then to pay attention to the cries of the marginalized and wounded people in the world and in their voices hear the call of God.

The third part of this assignment to help students arrive at a performative theology asks this question, "In what ways does the congregation participate in and fulfill the vocation of the church?" Entire books have offered a wide array of views on this question. Even so, this question can be addressed by way of considering three essential concepts: theological clarity, specific strategies, and an empowered congregation. Theological clarity, such as what is fostered by ongoing reflection on your credo, causes you to articulate what God desires for the world, as well as name those things in the church and community that undermine God's shalom and abundant life. With an understanding of what contributes to shalom and what subverts it, a congregation can then develop specific strategies that intentionally strengthen and deepen the community of faith and bless the world through well-defined and direct action. Every ambitious strategy is comprised of many somewhat modest, but exceptionally focused strategies. Congregations with theological clarity and specific strategies will already feel more empowered than will congregations without those things, of course. And members of a congregation who are squeezed into to pre-fitted, predetermined slots in an outdated organizational structure are rarely inspired to enact their theology. By contrast, members of an empowered congregation will have the time of their lives doing ministry. Indeed, an empowered congregation will affirm that people understand, experience, and emphasize the commitments of the gospel in diverse ways and will be encouraged to use their gifts and interests in ways that contribute to how they understand God's desire for the world.

The fourth part of this assignment asks students to consider one final question: "In light of God's desire for the world and how that shapes the vocation of the church, what is the particular role of the pastor?" The teaching of the pastor, which we will consider in the next chapter, helps the congregation focus on gospel priorities and ministry initiatives that both strengthen the congregation and bless the community. Most of those efforts require intentional, sustained leadership by the pastor and other church leaders. Your work as pastor is to continually be on the look out for ministry possibilities and then open hospitable spaces for joyful and hopeful conversations around what it means to be faithful in that particular time and place. Once possibilities for ministry are identified, you will be among those who keep those possibilities alive by way of facilitating increasingly concrete plans, weaving the gospel values that animate them into every possible conversation, and eventually systemizing a vision to the point that the congregation embraces these gospel-guided values and priorities.

Over time, mutual discovery, planning, and prioritizing occur between the pastor and the congregation. It is a spirit that prompts visions and dreams throughout the community of faith. Some of those dreams will take root and grow; others will remain lifeless in the ground, perhaps to come to fruition in another season. Both ministry that flourishes and ministry that falls flat provide rich opportunities for experimentation and learning. From that experimentation and learning comes a vibrant and compelling pastoral voice.

This four-part paper may begin as an assignment for a class, but it translates well to most congregational situations and deliberations that you will encounter in your ministry. In fact, it can transform many of those conversations. The spirit of a congregation changes when a few people in the church want to think in terms of what God desires of them and for the world, rather than simply reacting to the latest issue or perceived crisis. A congregation awakens, albeit slowly, to a purpose beyond its own needs and conveniences when it starts to think of its vocation as one that grows directly from what God desires for the world. At least a few discussions about a topic should shift at that point from interesting but detached studies to actionable dialogue that has something to say about how a congregation should spend its time, energy, and resources in ministry to the world. Once claimed by that realization, congregations can develop specific strategies to enact its beliefs and commitments. The pastor, as well as other congregational leaders, moves those conversations and projects along by asking thoughtful questions, relating the Christian story to given situations, encouraging new learning and risk taking, and offering support and comfort in difficult moments. Several of these conversations might occur at any given time, which then places the pastor in the role of weaving together the calling of the congregation and then seeing how the initiatives complement one another.

THE TERROR AND THE WONDER

It is a humbling experience to be asked, as Malcolm Warford was, what we believe and what differences our beliefs make in our lives. It can be unnerving to think that a congregation full of people will be watching us go about our ministry and, based on our words and actions, will draw their own conclusions about what we believe and whether those beliefs make any difference in our lives. But that is the nature of ministry. Whether in a meeting with three or four people planning spiritual life groups, or leading worship, or preaching at a funeral, or talking with a group of teenagers, or visiting with someone confined to her home, your understanding and experience of God will become somewhat evident to the people around you. It can be almost terrifying at times.

But there is a dimension of wonder to it as well. Do not let the wonder of such a public role be lost on you or your ministry. The Christian story gives life, so stay close to it and nurture it. Let others see the overflow of your own faith in those privileged moments of people's lives into which you, as a pastor, are invited.

Rev. Falwell performed his theology. So did Mother Teresa. So do countless people around the world. Simply, these are individuals whose convictions take concrete expression. With respect to the Christian story, your pastoral voice may begin with a credo, but it continues with the action that your credo calls forth from you. At its best, pastoral voice translates a profound theological clarity into specific faith commitments and focused ministry plans. From time to time, your congregation will catch a glimpse of what it looks like to enact their beliefs rather than just recite them. Thusly inspired, they may begin performing those beliefs for the sake of the world God loves so much. Those are incredibly exciting moments. Enjoy the wonder of those times.

4

Embracing the Vocation of Pastor

Don't ask yourself what the world needs. Ask yourself what makes you come alive and then go do that. Because what the world needs is people who have come alive.[1]

—HOWARD THURMAN

WE HAVE THIS MINISTRY

MINISTRY IS GROUNDED IN the shalom that God desires for the world. Ministry characterized by shalom is most evident in the life and example of Jesus of Nazareth. The work of a pastor is to hold that vision of shalom before the congregation such that congregational life and priorities grow out of the worship of God and focus on the healing of God's good world rather than, or at least in addition to, the inane activities and distractions that too often pass for the work of the church. Pastors accomplish this good work by maintaining integrity of faith and practice in their own lives and by faithfully fulfilling pastoral roles such as leading worship, teaching the faith, guiding congregational conversations, interpreting opportunities for mission and ministry, and caring for souls.

1. Bailie, *Violence Unveiled*, xv.

A call to ministry is not a mandate to maintain the status quo. Rather, this call is a mandate for change—more justice, more spirit, more compassion, more inclusiveness and more hope. However, those dreams, rooted in God's desire for the world, can get lost in the day-to-day and week-to-week activities of a minister or congregation that sees internal works and organizational maintenance as the reason for its existence rather than the means by which they accomplish their mission.

In practical terms, how does a minister help his or her congregation from losing its way? A preacher who presided over one particular ordination service presented the candidate with the following advice: "I can tell you that ministry is not a full-time job. No, it is a collection of part-time jobs, including but not limited to teacher, janitor, secretary, head of a small business, chaplain, worship leader, chief of personnel, planner, mail clerk, development officer, counselor, consultant, and a few others. And strangely enough, people in the congregations you will serve will not always agree about the proper way to prioritize these duties. Of course, not every congregation and not every person in the congregation will tell you what they expect of you."[2] In this sermon one can hear echoes of Joseph Sittler's description of vocational confusion that leads pastors to attempt far too many responsibilities that lie beyond the scope of pastoral work. Unable to meet these many complex expectations or to bear up to their emotional and mental drain, pastors often suffer from vocational guilt and personal depression. Sittler called it "the maceration of the minister."[3]

This preacher went on to speak clearly about what really constitutes pastoral work, but in this provocative opening he raised important questions: What do ministers do in a typical week? What will and will not claim your time? From whom or what will you take your cues? And what will characterize your ministry?

This chapter discusses the work of the pastor and the related field education opportunities that will help you develop your pastoral voice. The scope of ministry is vast and varied. We do not enter ministry fully grasping and finely executing its roles and responsibilities. Your pastoral voice will likely develop when you engage some part of ministry deeply enough to discover your authentic pastoral voice in that area, and then

2. Mooty, May 20, 2001.

3. Sittler, *Ecology of Faith*, 76–88.

allow that identity and practice to take root and grow in your other roles and responsibilities.

Ideally, you will be afforded a breadth of ministerial experience so that you can recognize your emerging voice in a variety of roles. You likely will recognize differences in your level of clarity, confidence, and comfort from one ministry role to the next. Perhaps at first you will feel more at ease in the pulpit than in the intensive care unit, or you might be clearer about your role when teaching than when leading a meeting, or you might be more confident when interpreting a ministry opportunity for the congregation than when praying during a worship service. The differences in clarity, confidence, and comfort provide you with important times of reflection. Ask yourself this simple question: What causes me anxiety in one moment and produces calm in another? Through repeated experience and reflection, your voice and presence will grow in all areas of ministry, but some of the anxiety may never completely disappear. In fact, some nervousness is good. More than just revealing our level of comfort or discomfort with certain roles, nervousness means that you are aware of the incredible moments in which you find yourself as a minister.

The primary context for pastoral work is the church. The church is called to be a life-giving community shaped by the life, death, and resurrection of Jesus wherein we have among us the same mind that was in Christ Jesus[4], make visible in our fellowship the realm of God,[5] and participate in God's purposes in the world. We engage a regular rhythm of coming together and being sent. We gather as a community for worship, learning, and fellowship. In those moments, we are nurtured to be a specific kind of community, one wherein God's extravagant diversity of gifts and perspectives is celebrated[6]. When we disperse, we do not simply leave the church building. We are sent. The church is a community of Jesus' followers who are called to continue the ministry of Jesus in the world by being his witnesses "in Jerusalem, in all Judea and Samaria, and to the ends of the earth."[7] Just as the word *apostle* refers to the one who is sent, so we, too, are sent into the community to love, heal, restore, and make whole. In doing so, the church participates in God's intended shalom for the world.

4. Phil 2:5.
5. Eph 3:10.
6. 1 Cor 12.
7. Acts 1:8.

Jesus calls us to God's vision for the world—to justice and mercy and faith.[8] And, thanks be to God, every once in a while a church claims those things as its guiding commitments. Every once in a while the life of Jesus and his tradition seep into our bones so deeply that we reawaken to the priorities of his life. Every once in a while the church becomes an environment where our lives can be transformed so that we can become agents of transformation for the sake of others. And when that happens, others recognize that we are looking beyond ourselves and the church's busyness and toward the shalom that God desires for us all.

Unfortunately, we do a lot in the church that shields us from God. We create and institutionalize distractions and then try to pass these distractions off as ministry. Indeed, at times it is a lot easier to create diversions, busily plan activities, and speculate about obscure biblical details that probably will never be answered than it is to have the mind of Christ Jesus in all we do and say, and then live as servants of justice, hospitality, peace, and reconciliation. Ministry is demanding work that calls us to feed the hungry, effect fairness, love the enemy, welcome the stranger, and practice peace. It is no wonder we go looking for other things to do. And these distractions may be fun things; but we should not confuse them with what Jesus has asked us to do. Institutional maintenance and administration are important aspects of ministry and church life, but an obsession with organizational reshuffling to the neglect of nurturing people in faith and blessing the community is not enough to sustain a congregation.

Thankfully, we know of congregations that participate in God's shalom. In these communities, God's all-embracing love is evident, encounters with God are pursued, members experience deep learning regularly, the adventure of faith causes people to think hopefully and imaginatively, and the church seeks to be a blessing both to the members and friends within and to the community around it. In the situations I have known of, there is one thing common to all of them: The group of leaders always includes a strong pastoral leader who is unrelenting and even annoying at calling the church back to its vocation of doing justice and being merciful and embodying a lively, hopeful faith. In every such situation that I know of, this strong pastoral leader refuses to be a good "company woman" or "company man" just for the sake of harmony and efficiency, and instead reports to the gospel, to the divine realm we see in Jesus.

8. Matt 23:23.

Different eras have emphasized different pastoral models: the scholar of the pre-nineteenth century, the pulpiteer of the nineteenth century, the builder of most of the twentieth century, and the manager of the late twentieth century.[9] William Willimon notes several ministerial models that hold sway today: the media mogul of televised worship, the political negotiator who engages structures and systems of power with the demands of the gospel, the therapist who seeks to ease anxiety and elevate spirits, the resident activist who moves about town agitating for reform, the preacher who reclaims the work of proclamation, and the servant who helps the servants of God understand the work to which they are called. These contemporary images remind us that ministry is so complex and multifaceted that no one single metaphor can capture completely and consistently a faithful understanding of pastoral work. Willimon offers a cautionary word to remind us that, as we think about these models, we should critique each for its countercultural aspects as related to the gospel, the extent to which each is grounded in Christian tradition and practice, and the level of responsiveness each has to the changing needs within the church and in the broader community.[10]

A minister can fall prey to many diversions and distractions while attempting to fulfill pastoral functions and satisfy a multitude of expectations. The variety of ministry energizes some pastors. No two days are alike. That same variety proves to be an overwhelming load of unfinished business and undue stress for other pastors. Along with the great variety of roles and responsibilities comes enormous freedom in determining how a pastor will spend his or her time, a freedom that many have not been able to bear.[11]

A key step in pastoral voice comes when ministers understand what work falls to them and what work belongs to the rest of the church. The work of the pastor is not more or less important than the work of congregation, but the pastor's work is specific. As the writer of Ephesians says, the body of Christ grows in faith and love through a variety of gifts and graces, including pastors and teachers whose work it is "to equip the saints for the work of ministry, for building up the body of Christ, until

9. See Hough and Cobb, *Christian Identity*, 5–16.
10. Willimon, *Pastor*, 56–74.
11. Proctor, *We Have This Ministry*, 55.

all of us come to the unity of the faith and of the knowledge of the Son of God, to maturity, to the measure of the full stature of Christ."[12]

It's not that pastors are set apart for privilege or prestige, rather they are called to do a particular work for which they are trained—to nurture a beloved community that can serve God's hope for the world. The result should not be an exalted pastor and a belittled congregation, but a whole community—pastor and congregation—claiming their voices and fiercely using their gifts as light to the world. When there is vocational confusion on the pastor's part, confusion ensues in the congregation about what should receive attention and energy. The pastor's role is to create an environment of hospitality that invites the congregation into rigorous conversations about what will characterize the life of the congregation and what will best embody the spirit and priorities of that character.[13] We, as pastors, are leaders at the point of our gifts and followers at the point of other people's gifts. This truism applies as much to the pastor as to anyone else in the congregation. A pastor whose work is continually distracted by a broken copier or who is unceasingly drawn into the details of newsletter creation or fundraising campaigns is a pastor who probably spends too much time tending to other such management details, which ultimately results in insufficient time for study, teaching, planning, and visioning.

We have a ministry, Paul tells the Christians in Corinth, by the mercy of God.[14] Ministry does not belong to one of us, but to all of us. I do not have this ministry alone, nor do you. We who are in the church have it together.

You are not the only one with a voice. Luke quotes Joel in saying that the spirit of God will be poured out on all flesh. As a result, sons and daughters will prophesy and many will see visions and dream dreams.[15] Likewise, a key part of the pastor's work is to help others in the community of faith find their voice. Pastors who insist that their voice and only their voice can express every dream and every authoritative word will not only stifle the gifts, visions, and dreams of those in their congregations, but also will find that their own voice is diminished. A theology of ministry grounded in the New Testament honors and nurtures the gifts of

12. Eph 4:12–13.
13. Hunter, *Desert Hearts*, 101.
14. 1 Cor 4:1.
15. Acts 2:17–18.

the whole community. A vital Christian witness depends on all of God's people offering themselves as living sacrifices in the hope that God's ways may prevail on earth as they do in heaven.

The church often uses the term "office" to think about what constitutes pastoral work. The office of pastor belongs to the church, and situates pastoral work in the life and purposes of the Christian tradition. The idea of office seeks to curb understandings that distort the relationship between the church and the pastor, such as minister as spiritual celebrity, religious entrepreneur, or autocratic authority. Unfortunately, office has not always guarded against the erosion of pastoral work into management and quasi-therapeutic models of ministry, nor has it protected pastoral work from some of the worst of the contemporary models and metaphors.

Denominations and church traditions vary in their understanding of office. For example, some traditions understand that ordination confers on ministers a sacramental authority that allows them to perform certain rites that the rest of the baptized cannot perform. On the other end of the spectrum are those traditions that ordain ministers for certain ministerial functions, many of which can be handled by any member of the congregation. Steve Sprinkle reflects this latter perspective when he writes of ministers affiliated with the Disciples of Christ: "The ordained have a particular ministry not different in kind, but distinctive in focus in equipping, nurturing, guiding, and setting before the church the ministry that is shaped by all.[16]

At the heart of this discussion is the conception and practice of ministry in ways that build up the body of Christ so that the church, in turn, blesses the wider community. The office of pastor seeks to do this by grounding ministers in pastoral wisdom and practices. The results of this approach are manifest: Preaching expresses more than personal opinion, caring for souls involves more than warm friendship, and hospitality depends on diverse partnerships rather than individual preferences and selective categories. Pastoral office defines the pastor's work as that of a leader of worship, as an interpreter of the faith, and as an equipper for ministry. Pastoral authority varies from tradition to tradition, but few expressions of this authority are more compelling than the holders of pastoral office who live authentic lives that are shaped by the life of Jesus and are focused on the purposes that God holds dear. By contrast,

16. Sprinkle, *Ordination*, 22.

few expressions of pastoral authority are more stifling than the use of the pastoral office to discourage other's gifts, ministries, and journeys of faith.

ENGAGING THE ROLES AND RESPONSIBILITIES OF MINISTRY

In the second sections of the two previous chapters, we discussed learning the truth of a place and articulating the truth of the gospel, respectively, and considered what truth is being called forth in you from each experience. This chapter asks you to think about the truth that is called forth in you as you engage a wide range of pastoral roles and responsibilities. By performing activities like preaching, baptizing, leading meetings, organizing ministry opportunities, and extending pastoral care, your field education experience will provide you with the opportunity to try on and live in various expressions of pastoral identity. You will claim some of these as your own, and some you will reject. You will refine many of these in some way as you discover what represents a compelling and authentic voice for you. This process will clarify your strengths and passion for ministry, help you understand how best to live and serve with your vulnerabilities, and engender a confident presence and a thoughtful practice of ministry.

In many supervised ministry programs, students are asked to develop a learning covenant with field education staff or supervisors at their seminary. Then, at their ministry sites, each student agrees to a job description whose final form, hopefully, reflects the student's own input and includes some overlap from the learning covenant. Your learning covenant and your job description may not become one, seamless statement, but you should be able to identify consistent themes and priorities between the two. Each should inform the other and, over time, lead you to possibilities to explore in each one that you did not consider when the two documents were first crafted.

A significant part of the responsibility for making explicit and continued connections between your learning covenant and your job description falls to you. Students invested in this process gain far more from it than those students who sit back and wait for insights and opportunities to come to them. The specifics for learning covenants and job descriptions vary among field education programs, but both the learning covenant and the job description should identify ways to help you develop your pastoral voice.

This section is divided into two lists. The first list offers guidelines you should consider when developing a job description and a learning covenant. The second list speaks briefly about areas of ministry in which you should seek significant amounts experience.

This first list to consider when developing an interlocked job description and a learning covenant includes the following five guidelines.

First, in terms of your learning covenant and your job description, you want each to include a healthy breadth of experience. The possibilities seem limitless, but often go unrealized. In almost every case, for seasoned students and novices alike, too many learning covenants are cautious, unimaginative, and uninspired. You should work with your supervisor to discover what you need to learn; but you must also consider what claims and energizes you for ministry, and then find ways to engage those things. Become an active learner now so that your ministry will be characterized by curiosity, imagination, and growth later.

Second, be as specific as possible about what you hope, want, and need to learn; and then commit your time to learn those things. Student ministry positions vary greatly. It will be a challenge for you to incorporate a breadth of pastoral experience into twelve or fifteen hours per week. To ensure a quality learning experience, you will need to be intentional about this process from the beginning, confer regularly with your supervisor about when to engage certain roles and responsibilities, revisit topics and issues from time to time for further discussion, and reflect on the ministry you have been doing. This level of intentionality will enhance your learning greatly. Without it, your field education experience will become a collection of weeks that do not add up to much.

Third, in addition to learning more about what you are specifically interested in, you must learn from your congregation. Your congregation will expect things from you. There will be times when congregational events require your leadership, support, and involvement, even though those events may not excite you at the moment. These are the times when the job description trumps the specifics of the learning covenant; but such events can provide a rich and important learning experience. Effective ministry means that you must engage in a wide variety of experiences. Indeed, you may not be profoundly enthused about all of them, now or after you graduate, but you should strive to do all of them with care, thoughtfulness, and excellence.

Fourth, identify one thing that is a particular passion for you and then look for avenues by which to pursue and express that passion. Given what you already know about your particular church and its congregation, do not assume that your passion is yours alone. You may be surprised. For example, I know of one student who while working in a consummately suburban church assumed that no one else in the congregation shared her passion for a rape crisis center. Yet, in that suburban church this student found several people who were looking for an opportunity to work in that area. If, however, you cannot incorporate your passion into the life of the congregation in any great degree, do not despair. Instead, look at this setback as a learning opportunity. Ask yourself why others in the congregation are not excited by your passion. Why have some passions gained traction among the priorities of your congregation's witness? Why does your passion fail to find support? How are you handling that? Can you find partners and possibilities in other places or do you give up on your passion?

And fifth, discover what experiences will stretch and challenge you. What in your field education experience will cause you to lean into your deficiency?[17] The trusted wisdom is to play to your strengths. But real learning happens when you reach beyond your familiar circles and delve into areas that you do not yet know or understand. Doing so likely will re-quire you to step into roles and situations that make you nervous, perhaps to the point of dread; but doing so will make your pastoral voice more complete. The writer's path offers a clear example of what it means to take such risks. Laraine Herring says that most failed writing attempts can be traced back to the absence of personal risk in the effort. "The writer tries to play it safe, tries to couch what he's doing in layers of deep, and often beautifully phrased crap. . . . But the risk of writing is an internal risk. You brave the depths of your own being and then, oh my, bring it back up for commentary by the world. Not the work of wimps."[18]

This second list offers a brief description of the five areas that repre-sent a breadth of ministry experience. It will be of benefit to engage each of these areas to some degree, have the chance to reflect on them with

17. Heifetz, *Practice of Adaptive Leadership*, 252.
18. Herring, *Writing Begins with the Breath*, 16.

your supervisor and a support committee within the congregation. With some, however, you may not have extensive exposure and experience. In those cases, you still will have the chance to reflect on how your supervisor or other pastors approach these areas and to think intentionally about how you will engage them later in your own ministry.

The first area is planning and leading worship. Worship is central to congregational life: it focuses and grounds each member's shared life in God. Moreover, worship provides a uniquely visible moment for you as a ministry student. Many opportunities exist in the area of worship to explore your pastoral voice and your own becoming. These opportunities include the congregation's regular weekly worship service(s), but also include episodic services that are shaped by the liturgical year, local custom, or unanticipated events. Try to take part in both the planning and the performance of as many different parts of the worship service as much as is possible. While many individuals may meet and work with you at different times in smaller groups, it is in worship that the whole congregation exercises its collective eye and sees you. When you play an active particular role in worship, you are helping members of the congregation confirm you in your place among them. After all, not just anybody is asked to lead worship. Remember also that people will encounter you in other settings, within and beyond the congregation, and will relate to you, at least to some degree, based on how they actually experience your leadership roles related to worship.

The second area is teaching the faith in a variety of settings and with various groups. Teaching is central to pastoral work, and pastoral ministry is filled with occasions that allow you to help people of faith (and doubt) understand and live more fully into what it means to be a child of God and a follower of Jesus. Whether people are gathering for worship, or Bible study, or fellowship, or ministry planning, they want to know, to borrow King Zedekiah's question of Jeremiah, if there is any word from the Lord[19] in the midst of journeys filled with questions, dilemmas, and opportunities. In and out of church, we encounter competing stories that generate feelings of hope, dissonance, and conflict within us. Stories shape who we are; yet they also compete for our allegiance.

The pastor is a resident theologian, a lead interpreter of the faith, who brings into every conversation what it means for individuals and

19. Jer 37:17.

congregations to live faithfully today as followers of Jesus Christ. A congregation may or may not grant a pastor a lot of authority on some things, but interpreting the faith is a key aspect and expectation of pastoral ministry. The congregation authorizes a pastor to teach, by virtue of his or her office. When you consistently perform well in this area, members of your congregation likely think more deeply on what it means to be the church. Over time, they may even think of you as someone who speaks with authority on matters of faith. If so, it is one sign that you are discovering your pastoral voice.

The third area is caring for the congregation. As with worship and teaching, opportunities for care present themselves to a pastor in various forms and times. Students who are solo pastors likely will encounter many opportunities to offer pastoral care. It will be harder for student associate ministers and ministerial interns to get involved in pastoral care, largely because congregants have existing relationships with the pastor and others. But it is not impossible for students in such situations to gain firsthand experience in providing such care. In addition to accepting invitations into certain individual and family situations, students can visit with people who are confined to their home or nursing home, make hospital calls, share in wedding planning, and participate in funerals. Students also have the chance to offer pastoral care when they are present with others from the church in worship services, fellowship events, mission efforts in the community, and so forth.

Students can experience other aspects of pastoral care through shepherding a congregation through controversy and conflict that surface either in the congregation itself or the wider community. Opportunities for you to provide pastoral care occur when you minister to individuals after surgery, before a funeral, in advance of a wedding, or during a divorce. Members of your congregation also need and depend on pastoral care when they are they are dealing with divisive issues where people take sides. The pastor is among those leaders who shepherd the congregation through difficult conversations and challenging moments. Many students will not be ready for an experience like this, and most congregations will not expect them to be involved, but you will enhance your pastoral voice by being aware of such situations, observing how others work through them, and then reflecting with a supervisor on how you might handle these moments.

The fourth area is attending to congregational administration that supports the church's vocation. The mention of meetings, budgets, staff oversight, committee work, and follow-through does not generate a lot of enthusiasm for many people. Perhaps these people have never seen congregational administration done well, or perhaps it remains unclear to them how such activities can support and enliven a church's ministry. Your learning will benefit if you work with a pastor and a congregation who weave every administrative conversation and initiative with theological clarity and ministerial priorities. In such an environment, you will be able to see how congregational administration functions for the sake of a church's mission and witness.

As with pastoral care, your access to some areas of congregational administration may be rather limited. Lobby for as many opportunities as is possible for you, and then observe the areas that you cannot participate in directly. And as always, find times to reflect with your supervisor and others in areas such as preparation, process, stakeholders, goals, content, and outcomes. Once serving in a congregation, seminary graduates often regret not getting involved with matters of congregation administration during their field education experience. Areas of particular importance for you are in leading meetings, working with boards and councils, developing budgets, supervising staff, casting a vision, and moving an initiative through the system. While these administrative areas can be discussed in the seminary classroom and in workshops after seminary, there is no substitute for engaging these areas in the particular context of a congregation's dreams, plans, conflicts, and baggage.

The fifth area that is represented in the breadth of ministry experience is interpreting opportunities for mission in the local and global context. Pastors do not simply preside over a congregation, especially these days when few things hold still long enough to be presided over. Pastors employ their own vocational clarity and the theological clarity of the congregation to look for ways that the congregation can claim its calling and live into its ministry. In the past, many congregations entered into strategic planning processes that established their objectives and goals for a three to five year span. A more recent approach to mission, which has resonated with some congregations, is that of understanding their story, identifying what they believe to be the core values of the gospel, and then charging a group of people to be continually on the alert for ways to live out those values. Some opportunities will excite and energize certain members in a congregation. Likewise, other members will not feel the pull of those particular opportunities. As people discern a call to certain ministries, either in the local context or around the world, a congregation might enact specific strategies and pursue them so that a difference can be made in the world. Without action all planning is talk, and energized people will go elsewhere—often to a non-church group or agency—to use their gifts in the remaking of God's world.

For example, congregations that are claimed by the Bible's insistence on hospitality will introduce specific measures to demonstrate hospitality in a variety of ways. Congregations that are outraged by environmental degradation might offer detailed and explicit approaches for change—approaches through which people can actionably offer themselves and their expertise to these ministries. Remember, vagueness is always on the side of the status quo. If pastors or small groups do not offer specific and detailed plans for action, from the beginning of an idea to its engagement and follow-through, little will change, and the frustration level of a congregation will go through the roof.

Ideally, the pastor is not the only person who keeps vigilant watch for opportunities for mission and interpreting faithful expressions of core values. However, the pastor plays a leadership role in this aspect of ministry, and for this reason a clear pastoral voice is critical for successfully transforming opportunities into action and change. You, as a student pastor, bring something to the congregation that is invaluable—the energy of someone who has just begun a ministry and a fresh set of eyes to see what is possible. As you learn more about your context and congregation, you will be able to make more and more connections between the congregation's core values and opportunities for ministry. Depending on your role and what is going on in the congregation at the time, it may be appropriate for you, as a student, to share some connections you are particularly curious about. Your supervisory sessions are ideal times to talk about the possibilities you see. A supervisor who is committed to your learning experience will explore those with you and perhaps will help you discover how you can effectively share your observations with other leaders at your church.

HOW DOING MINISTRY GIVES RISE TO PASTORAL VOICE: SOME CASE STUDIES

Two case studies follow that show how engaging in various pastoral roles and responsibilities at your ministry site can clarify your vocational path and animate your pastoral voice.

Mary Jane and the Revelation to John

Mary Jane was not excited about beginning her field education experience. She believed she was called to military chaplaincy and did not think that spending a year in a congregation as a pastoral intern would be necessary or helpful to her. She described her anticipated vocational path to the dean of her seminary and appealed to have her field education requirement waived, but she was instead given several examples of how field education would contribute to her ministry as a chaplain. Mary Jane reluctantly agreed to undertake the internship.

When Mary Jane began as a pastoral intern at St. Andrew's Church, she did so with moderate resistance and low expectations. Later, she would discover that those expectations were colored by some personal issues that likely would impact her ministry well into the future. In the midst of processing some of those expectations, Mary Jane realized that she held some very compelling faith positions; but her nervousness about speaking in public had caused her to minimize and disregard her convictions. She essentially had chosen military chaplaincy because she thought that most of her ministry in that role would be confined to one-to-one encounters, which in turn would allow her to avoid the nerve-racking moments of leading groups in worship and study.

Mary Jane's supervisor, Pastor Dan, rather quickly disabused her of this notion. His ten years of experience as a chaplain in Iraq provided a credible counter to her assumptions. Mary Jane came to understand that in order become an effective military chaplain, she needed to deal with a couple of issues—and that her field education experience would allow her that chance. Pastor Dan provided invaluable practical insight into in what the day-to-day work of a military chaplain looks like, and helped Mary Jane discern whether or not this aspect of ministry was her calling. Second, at St. Andrew's she was given ample opportunity to find her voice in public settings and larger groups.

A particularly formative series of events occurred for Mary Jane while she prepared for and led a Bible study on the last book of the New Testament, the Revelation to John. She had completed a course on Revelation at her seminary, but she was perfectly content to let the issues raised in that book remain at school. Her supervising pastor, who regularly taught about difficult biblical stories and controversial social issues, encouraged Mary Jane to offer a six-week study at her church on what many consider to be the most perplexing book in the Bible.

Mary Jane believed that this complex book offered a timely and hopeful word to today's Christians; but she was very nervous about how her understanding of Revelation would be received by members of the congregation at St. Andrew's. She expected strong disagreement from two different groups: those who claimed that the book includes literal predictions and easily recognized signs of the soon-to-be end times, and those who long ago dismissed Revelation as the account of a hallucinogenically induced vision that has only been used to harm other people and divert attention away from more concrete and pressing problems. Mary Jane knew that, unlike most Bible studies at her church, this one would generate a lot of interest and that both camps would be well represented. She was concerned about articulating her views and responding to questions and challenges.

During that six-week study, there were not many converts. The Fundamentalists were still pinning the title of the "the Beast" on their most despised political and entertainment figures. The liberals continued to think the graphic nature and bewildering details could only be attributed to one toke too many. Those at the interpretative extremes of the conversation did not budge much, but those in the theological middle found the class to be exceptionally informative and compelling.

In the first couple of sessions, Mary Jane fielded questions very tentatively, almost defensively at times. But her reticence gradually gave way to confidence over the course of those six weeks. Each week she experienced increased energy during her preparation. Each week of teaching enhanced her own understanding of this often misunderstood book. By the third week, she was responding to questions and comments graciously and forthrightly. Instead of viewing everyone in the group as being someone who was eagerly looking for a chance to dispute her approach to Revelation and to question her claims, Mary Jane saw the members of her class for who they were—people searching for a better understanding of an important part of the Biblical witness. This insight allowed her to calmly describe the book of Revelation as being a relevant and encouraging word for any group of marginalized or oppressed Christians. She had done well in her seminary class on Revelation, but not until she heard herself teaching did she become aware of what was rising within her. It was through the central pastoral role of teaching that Mary Jane began to identify and exercise her pastoral identity. She experienced a level of comfort and clarity while teaching that she had not known when performing other pastoral roles and responsibilities. Those in the study group took notice of the way in which her pastoral voice was emerging in their midst. Moreover, the clarity and confidence that Mary Jane had claimed through teaching became increasingly evident in other areas of her ministry, such as the leadership of worship, pastoral care, administration, and local missions.

Mary Jane's positive and successful field education experience left her with meaningful questions about the nature of her pastoral voice. Should she interpret the fulfillment and enjoyment of teaching as an invitation to rethink her previous rejection of congregational ministry? Or did her passion and energy still lie with military chaplaincy, and had her intern experience simply helped her become better prepared for that particular work? What other pastoral roles and responsibilities could she engage in thoroughly enough to help her answer these questions? Were there ways to serve as a pastor and a chaplain at the same time? Was she unnecessarily and prematurely narrowing her vocational path at this point? Mary Jane sensed that exploring these and other questions would yield important discoveries. She was surprised, but also grateful, to discover that a congregational setting offered her the space and opportunities for that exploration.

Rodney the Piano Man

Some people thought Rodney was a prodigy. At age four he first sang in the Christian Methodist Episcopal Church. Two years later he provided piano accompaniment for two Easter Sunday morning anthems. People marveled at his incredible talent. They pondered the opportunities that Rodney might have at some point in his life. Rodney does not remember feeling undue pressure, but he reports overhearing adults having conversations about him, and he remembers being aware that his life was a frequent topic of conversation.

Despite his talents, Rodney enjoyed a remarkably well-rounded adolescence—he was socially connected, athletic, intellectually curious, and yes, musically gifted. During his college years, he became involved in a congregation in the town where he attended school. After completing degrees in piano and voice, Rodney returned to his home church and became the minister of music, a half-time position he held while teaching high school music and giving private lessons. Under his leadership, the music and arts program flourished at his church. As one might imagine, the congregation was ecstatic to have him back home and serving in this role. Rarely was there a Christian Methodist Episcopal (C.M.E.) district assembly or national convocation that Rodney was not asked to plan and lead the music.

Rodney could not imagine music not being a part of his life. At the same time, he felt a call to a broader ministry. This call pointed him toward a life that was not being exclusively defined by music. Answers to the questions that surfaced would drastically impact his family and congregation, but first he needed to explore these questions on his own. How did he presently understand his call to ministry? He wondered about this. How did he see his vocational path unfolding from here? He could not yet say.

The answers to these questions were clouded by the changes and losses that he knew would occur if he were to think seriously about preparing for pastoral work. For example, what if he attended seminary and then was appointed as the pastor of a local congregation? What would his role be in that congregation with regard to the music ministry? The chances were good that he might be more talented and better trained for music leadership than anyone else in the congregation. Would he need to let go of his music interests altogether? Or could his time and energy be split between roles that traditionally fall to the pastor and the music leadership? Just as important, how interested was he in leaving his home congregation and the people who had supported him from the time he was a very young boy?

Rodney thought that taking a class at a local seminary might clarify some issues for him, and so he enrolled in a class called Introduction to the New Testament. He enjoyed the class, and decided to continue his studies. However, in the following semester, the only class that fit with his schedule was one called Pastoral Care and Counseling. At first he thought he would sit out that term because the class did not interest him very much, but he changed his mind at the last minute and registered on the day of the first class. The first few assignments asked him to visit specific places, observe what happened in those spaces, and then write a brief reflection on each experience. To begin, Rodney attended an open Alcoholics Anonymous meeting. The following week he sat for two hours in the main lobby of a major hospital. After that, he secured permission to accompany his pastor to visit one person in her home and one person in a nursing home.

This portion of the semester concluded with a Sunday morning assignment. Students were to look out upon the worshipping congregation and note the changes and transitions in people's lives of which the students were aware. From his seat near the choir loft, as inconspicuously as possible, he jotted down the changes of people's lives that he knew of—relocation of a family, death of a sister, job loss, transition to assisted living, divorce, change in school districts, noticeable decline in mental alertness, new parents holding their baby, work promotion, downsizing in living arrangements. He recorded twenty-seven changes and transitions in people's lives just by casually looking out on the worshipping community that day. In addition to these individual changes and family transitions, the congregation itself had elected new leadership and was dealing with significant shifts in the neighborhood around the church.

Prior to this assignment, Rodney had not given this level of personal and communal flux much thought. Now, in thinking about this reality, he found himself thinking about the role of pastor as one who shepherds people and congregations through the wide scope of human joy and pain. He wondered if this might be a signpost for his unfolding vocational journey. Out of this discernment came a new appreciation for how the music of the church spoke to the celebrations and challenges of people's lives and how, with his background, that could be woven into pastoral ministry in fresh ways.

A call to pastoral ministry swelled within him. Rodney talked with the pastor and other leaders at his church about expanding his role beyond the music ministry. Though the leadership team was concerned that Rodney might look elsewhere if they did not reconfigure his responsibilities, they were mostly puzzled by what they viewed to be an unnecessary and somewhat disruptive request. A few members of Rodney's church recognized and nurtured Rodney's call, but they did so with this caveat: "You will not be able to explore this in your home congregation," they told him. "Our needs and perceptions simply won't give you enough room." Rodney continued at the church for another year, but he was encouraged to seek out ministry opportunities in a congregation that interested him.

So, instead of enrolling full-time at the nearby seminary where he had taken one class per semester for two years, Rodney and his family moved five states away to a place where they knew practically no one. That was the bad news. Their network of support no longer lived down the street and around the corner. But the move also brought good news. A gracious space had opened in which they could explore the new life that stretched before them and begin to live more fully because of it. Some of Rodney's questions remained, as did some of his fears and doubts. But the spiritual roominess generated the energy and excitement he and his family needed to live hopefully with those concerns, and Rodney was able to engage his call and pastoral ministry in the broadest ways possible as the solo pastor of the C.M.E. congregation a few miles from their new home.

CULTIVATING VOICE: RISKING THE POSSIBILITIES OF MINISTRY

In chapter two of this book we considered one part of the story in Matthew 10. Let us now pay attention to a different theme from that same story. Jesus calls together twelve disciples to send them into a world that is full of possibility and pain. Jesus announces, "The kingdom of heaven—the hope and nearness of God for you and me, all of God's children, and all creation—has come near."[20] And then he gives instructions that are ambitious and clear: "Proclaim the good news, cure the sick, raise the dead, cleanse the lepers, cast out demons."

Jesus had already noted the need for more people to participate in what God desires for the world.[21] At this point, I cannot help but wonder if Jesus said something like, "So friends, are you with me on this? Are the deep longings and various gifts of your lives also claimed by this work? Will you put yourself out there on the line, with me, to ease people's suffering and to shine some of God's light in the world?"

20. Matt 10:7.
21. Matt 9:37–38.

That's moving quickly and getting right to the point, isn't it? Perhaps he should have first let the disciples serve on the set-up committee for the "fellowship hour" as a way of easing them into things. Instead, what we hear is Jesus calling and entrusting these disciples with God's most essential work: "Cure the sick, raise the dead, cleanse the lepers, cast out demons." These were specific and, we would think, rather daunting instructions. What's more, these instructions were "iffy."

It's right there in the story, that little word that can halt plans and stall dreams. *If.* Jesus sends the disciples on a bold mission, but as he wraps up the instructions he slips in something at the end. *If.* Jesus says, "If anyone will not welcome you or listen to your words . . ."

We wonder how the disciples heard that *if.* "What did he say?" somebody must have asked. "Is that all the assurance we get? If?"

The word *if* gives individuals and congregations pause today when an important and joyful work promises no guarantee for success. In those "iffy" moments we realize again that adventurous faith and fulfilling ministry take us directly through risky situations. The disciples may have experienced something similar.

The editorial heading above this passage in some Bibles calls it "The Mission of the Twelve." In one respect, that is exactly what this story is about—the disciples being sent to "cure the sick, raise the dead, cleanse the lepers, and cast out demons." But more is happening here than simply Jesus' instructions for how the disciples should minister to others. Part of what goes unmentioned in this story is how the disciples themselves will be changed as a result of their ministry experiences. They will experience significant moments of learning as they make this ministry their own. By immersing themselves in the work that Jesus had entrusted to them, the twelve are about to discover who they were becoming as followers of Jesus and as instruments of God's shalom.

Jesus essentially says to his disciples, "You have been with me; you have heard my teaching; you know my story; you have seen my work. I have demonstrated what lies at the heart of God and now it's your time to claim this way of life in your own thinking and speaking and living." The only way these words of Jesus are made real is when we, each of us, goes out on our own, like baby birds being pushed out of the nest to fly, like a tight-rope artist working above the crowd without the benefit of a net, like beginning a journey with no confirmation numbers and no sixty-day guarantees. As daunting as that can be, it is in those moments that faith grows within us, stretches our imagination, animates our gifts and talents, and guides us toward a self-understanding as people in ministry.

The path of ministry, as with most of life, takes us through uncertain times and terrain where even the smallest of words can construct the greatest of obstacles. What we often miss is that risky moments and iffy situations can also hold the most germane and fulfilling possibilities. We want to position ourselves spiritually and emotionally in such a way as to be able to decide whether anxiety or possibility will hold the greatest attraction, and whether fear or hope will characterize our lives and ministry. Calculation and timidity inhibit many pastoral leaders and the congregations they serve. Others, though, are energized by possibilities, risk-laden as they are.

A key factor in determining the quality of a field education experience is directly related to the amount of real responsibility that a congregation and supervising pastor entrusts to their student pastor. Students must encounter at least some of the risks that are inherent in ministry. Your field education experience will be enhanced when a supervisor and congregation grant you a meaningful amount of latitude and freedom to explore your pastoral voice. Some of your learning will come from missteps and mistakes. Good supervising pastors and congregations understand this. They also understand that in order for you to discover and claim pastoral voice means that you must take some chances, risk failure, and experience vulnerability. In pastoral encounters, whether in leading worship, caring for others, or interpreting ministry opportunities, we risk misunderstanding, disagreement, rejection, dismissal, hostility, and indifference, just to name a few. Only those students who are highly motivated to grow in their ministerial effectiveness will recognize the value of these risks and remain present to the ways they might rearrange and stretch their self-understanding and practice of ministry.

If you are a solo student pastor, there are few places in the congregation to hide from real responsibility and real risks. You are highly visible as a regular preacher and teacher, as the one person to call in times of crisis, and as the one who is enmeshed in most every aspect of the congregation's life. The challenge you will face as a student is ensuring that the church you serve sees itself as a teaching congregation, and so intentionally carves out opportunities that allow you to affirm your ministry and provides you with timely, constructive feedback.

Student associate ministers and interns are confronted with a different challenge. Simply, you may be able to slip into the background, and in so doing allow yourself to be far less engaged than you should be. Slipping into the background does not help you discover your pastoral voice. Your field education experience is your opportunity to take advantage of the relatively safe and supportive environment of a ministry site, to move from observing ministry to doing ministry, from standing in the safety and shadows of someone else's leadership to stepping out on your own and leading. Without the emotional force that risk generates, your learning will be diminished.

In ministry, the risks are many. We will encounter and participate in a spectrum of human experience that is stunningly broad and deep. Some of these experiences catch even seasoned pastors by surprise and cause them to ask questions like, "What do I say and what do I do?" For both students and seasoned pastors, the absence of readily available answers can cause anxiety and frustration, especially when it feels like the eyes of the congregation are upon them. That said, there is no substitute for a strong pastoral voice when the ready-made responses can sound trite, irrelevant, and uncaring.

Insights from coursework, mentors, and your own life and faith will inform each pastoral moment you face. Even so, much of your learning about what to say and do occurs as you live and serve in the midst of intensely specific situations. In the times you are practicing ministry, you should be reflecting on your practice. You should carefully interpret what is happening or has happened, and prayerfully determine what constitutes a faithful witness on your part, even as you are already offering ministry to those people involved.

The following are some other examples of risk that can help foster your pastoral voice. First, your pastoral identity will be enhanced by daring to lead when it's not clear that others will follow. In some cases, you will be asked to oversee established ministries that already enjoy congregational support. When possible, it is beneficial to develop and undertake a new ministry project whose success is not guaranteed. This may allow you to experience what leadership feels like and learn from the congregation's enthusiastic or tepid reception to what you have proposed and implemented. Another risk occurs as you begin to build relationships with people in the church you are serving. The promise of those budding friendships and partnerships is off the charts, but the ways in which human relationships can sour, sometimes rather quickly, seem almost limitless as well. Another risk is that of success. The realization that we actually can preach particularly good sermons, or lead effective Bible study discussions, or generate enthusiasm and participation for a ministry project, can be startling. Mark Hart notes that he has observed otherwise motivated seminary students resist and even sabotage their own growth because it means "a change of behavior, paradigm, or a change of relationship with others."[22] Still another risk comes into play when, as a result of your study and observation, you begin to envision ways to strengthen the congregation's life and presence in the community. Worthwhile dreams can experience a lot of criticism and revision before ever coming close to materializing. A lot of dreamers have recognized that price, and so have chosen to remain quiet. Others have taken risks and have discovered a way of being in ministry that is treacherous, yet energizing and brimming with possibilities for growth.

Listen to the way poet Stephen Dunn describes the risk-taking of his craft:

> A person can die if there's no departure from the known place. Therefore, I've learned that I need, now and then, to get myself in a little trouble. Insert a foreign detail. Say something I can't yet support, or even fully understand. In a sense, to step out of my neighborhood. If I'm not lost after I've gotten lost, I may have something to talk about and a new place from which to say it."[23]

Dunn captures both the necessary experience and desired outcome for theological field education. If you are serious about cultivating and discovering your pastoral voice, now and then you will need to live just beyond where your scripts function well, beyond where your existing skills suffice, and beyond the experiences that allow your current identity to remain intact. From time to time you will need to step out of that neighborhood of understanding long enough to encounter that which is new and different. It can be hugely beneficial to get lost a few times, to feel like you are in over your head, especially while you are still in a relatively supportive environment like a teaching congregation. Some foreign detail, as Dunn describes it, may change your practice of ministry. Even if it does not, such an experience will expand your view of life and ministry so

22. Hart, "Focusing Upon Skill Development," 10.
23. Dunn, *Walking Light*, 11.

that you can better embrace your own perspective and practice with new vitality. If so, your ministry will really have something to say, something that others cannot help but consider because of its force of newness and insight.

Most of the time there is no recipe, no road map. There are only compelling possibilities that stir our souls. Then we must decide whether to play it safe, push down those stirrings, and go with what we already know, or sign up for a cause and devote our lives to it, risks and all.

5

Discovering Who You Are as a Person in Ministry

What a long time it takes to become the person one has always been![1]

—PARKER PALMER

The very least you can do in your life is to figure out what you hope for. And the most you can do is live inside that hope. Not admire it from a distance but live right in it, under its roof.[2]

—BARBARA KINGSOLVER

WHEN THE PERSON IN MINISTRY IS YOU

I ONCE ATTENDED A workshop that was designed to improve supervision skills. The participants came mostly from chaplaincy and field education departments, but a few congregational ministers also attended. Most of us probably expected to receive something like an updated supervisor's tool kit that included the latest thinking on supervision, some innovative supervisory techniques, information about recent changes in employment

1. Palmer, *Let Your Life Speak*, 9.
2. Kingsolver, *Animal Dreams*, 334.

laws, and so forth. Breanne, a Clinical Pastoral Education (CPE) supervisor, approached the day's announced topic differently. After dividing the class into small groups, she gave us the first of several startling discussion questions. "What," Breanne began, "is the truest thing that can be said about you?"

The question hung in the air as we sat there; we did not know each other very well. And, at least for some of us, the first thoughts that came to mind stuck in our throats like an inaudible blockage.

For Breanne, that question is the starting point for thinking about who we are as people in ministry. She believes that every person preparing to be a pastor or chaplain has to come to grips with this question in order to do that work well. She contends that these professionals are not ready to serve and supervise others until they can articulate an honest answer.

Laraine Herring captures this sentiment in this way: "When we as writers talk about finding our voices, we mean: What do I sound like when there is nothing and no one else speaking? What do I have to say once the distractions of my life are stilled?"[3] She notes that writers often try changing locations in hope of finding a less cluttered place; but many of them become very frustrated when they realize—if they realize—that their distractions and contradictions have followed them. These writers carry their burdens everywhere they go, that is, until they find a way to be still and simply listen.

Ministers can experience a similar phenomenon. More than a few of us attempt to sustain a frenetic pace, often in an effort to avoid quiet moments and discerning introspection. We pack days with activities, events, and meetings. We organize weeks to preclude a Sabbath and the possibility of knowing God in the stillness. We think in terms of professional careers and congregational successes. We structure our work in ways to give the impression of always running toward something—some goal, some need, some opportunity. Upon reflection, however, one cannot help but wonder if we are really at the same time running away from something, perhaps from what *is* the truest thing about us. Perhaps we are concerned that if we slow down people in the congregation will know what we already know about ourselves. I hate to break this news to you, but my guess is that they already know. Like us, members of a congregation may resist

3. Herring, *Writing Begins with the Breath*, 114.

claiming the truest things about their own lives, but most of them will recognize the joys and sorrows, the hopes and the demons, that their pastor carries. Our busyness puts these truths on center stage for everybody to see, except us. Many people in ministry—and, for that matter, in every other vocation—struggle with the complexity of human personalities and the web of human motivations. Within each of us are all sorts of voices that clamor for attention and allegiance, and their cries can surface at the most inopportune times. Strange combinations of passion and reason clash over the direction of our lives. What excites us about ministry one week may be a huge source of frustration the following week. While in a meeting, we may overreact one minute to someone's innocent and innocuous comment, and the next minute offer the wisdom of the ages. Only later, upon reflection, might we probe into the unresolved emotional issues that hooked us and caused such emotional reactions.

Ministry is emotionally and spiritually demanding. We find ourselves in raw moments of pain and loss, as well as in exhilarating moments of joy and celebration. A day may start with a visit to a hospice unit and finish in the nursery of the same hospital. In between, we may have led a conversation about crime and racial equality in the community, participated in a discussion about the priorities of the church budget, carved out a couple of hours of worship planning and sermon preparation, and taught a Bible study with a group of teenagers. None of these settings may have been maliciously conflicted, but the potential for conflict is a given whenever two or more people are present. And sometimes we carry enough internal conflicts to make that second person completely unnecessary.

Counseling professors often ask therapists in training, "What is becoming a therapist doing to you?" Through students' own therapy and their practicum experiences of being a therapist, their own personal issues bubble up. Part of the learning in that setting comes from paying attention to what is emerging and how it is presenting itself in one's life, and then note what is being activated and how it is manifesting itself in the therapeutic practice. The hope, of course, is that therapists will become more aware of their own needs and issues so that they do not impose them on their clients. Engaging in real-life, real-time ministry at your field education site has a way of surfacing fears, wounds, and motivations that you may not be aware of normally, or at least do not have to deal with on a regular basis.

So what is becoming a pastor doing to you? What are you discovering about your strength and fragility, your confidence and anxiety, your capacity for love and betrayal, as you step into ministerial roles and pastoral situations? Ministers consider this question for the same reason therapists do. Coming to grips with a call to pastoral ministry can cause all sorts of things to surface. Some may be very exciting. An equal number may be quite troubling. Some issues may arise that only therapy can provide you with an adequate space to explore them. In any event, we do not tidy up our lives and tie up all our loose ends before we enter ministry. Instead, we become aware of our issues and work through them as best we can. With this awareness, we claim the value of our various journeys and experiences, including difficult moments and disappointing events, and allow those experiences to deepen our understanding and broaden our perspective.

I have taught a course for students in their first semester of seminary called, "Spirituality, Autobiography, and Ministry." In this class each student reads a different spiritual classic and then makes a presentation about the turning points in the author's spiritual journey, how the author has experienced God, and how that encounter with God made a difference in the person's spirit and priorities. Over the course of the semester, students become acquainted with many spiritual classics and, in the process, cannot help but note that no two paths are alike. They find points of resonance with some and not with others. Considering the similarities and the differences help students to clarify their own paths. Class members reinforce their learning over a semester's time as they begin to talk about the pivotal moments, influential people, and particular circumstances of their own lives. When students recognize that no two paths are alike they become more comfortable with their own journeys.

Writer Patrice Vecchione says that our culture suffers from "a negation of the inner self."[4] We end up living rather flat lives at best, and sometimes we live out of a distortion of ourselves. The unimaginative flattening of communities described in chapter two of this book happens to individuals as well. We tend to accept group-thought and mirror group feelings instead of considering who we really are, and then mustering the nerve to live out of that identity.[5] You cannot give yourself to ministry if

4. Vecchione, *Writing and the Spiritual Life*, 14.
5. Rohr, *Contemplation in Action*, 132.

you cannot be yourself. Further, you will not be experienced by others as giving yourself to ministry if you are not being yourself. And yet, it takes no small amount of work to discover, understand, and claim the essence of your own person in ministry. Hopefully, you will move into ministry with some ideas of what drives and disturbs you. A good field education experience will provide numerous opportunities that allow you to clarify further your life's hope and its tender places.

At your center, who are you and how are you expressing that through your ministry? A woman in Bombay (now Mumbai), India, once made a critical distinction. She said, "In America you know everything about personality but almost nothing about essence. Here in India we know much about essence and hardly bother with personality."[6] To ask ourselves what is the truest thing that can be said about us is not an attempt to embarrass or dredge up a painful memory—though there is no guaranteed protection from either of those—but to discover again the true nature of our essence. To do ministry well we need to know where our truest self resides, and then consistently live from that center, regardless of what is going on around us. Those individuals who need to have everything in place so that their lives can be manageable—who need the stars to line up just so in order for them to engage in ministry—usually do not handle ministry's weekly unpredictability and creative chaos very well. On the other hand, those with a strong sense of self live and serve in the midst of all kinds of craziness with exceptional clarity, resiliency, and focus.

I would be remiss not to mention that, tragically, some congregations and denominations do not make room for people to be themselves in any circumstance, and especially not in ordained ministry. The church has found stunning and persistent ways to demean people. If imagination of that degree could be channeled toward goodness and healing, the church would be expressed and experienced differently. Instead, too often the church has marginalized and even blatantly excluded the very people whose faith, gifts, and energy could lead to a greater measure of faithfulness. The church should be the realm where all of us have an opportunity to find the voice and the nerve to effect justice for all of God's children.

Perhaps the catchphrase for the National Clergy Renewal Grants can help us think about what lies at the heart of our lives and ministry. In this

6. Ibid., 123.

program, sponsored by the Lilly Endowment,[7] applicants are encouraged to respond to the question, "What makes your heart sing?" Each of us will answer that question differently, and the response may change somewhat from season to season, but articulating an answer to that question is a way of thinking about our essence. In doing so, we open our lives and begin to trust that which is within us already and allow it to claim our energies.

We know what happens when the needs and wounds of ministers play out in a congregation: Anger alienates the congregation and undermines pastoral effectiveness. Their individual emotional needs cloud conversations and create widespread role confusion. The lack of self-acceptance leads to trying to control and even fix others. Insecurity obstructs otherwise thoughtful plans and good intentions Depression distorts a minister's perception and blurs his or her boundaries. Family of origin issues surprise and ensnare. Anxiety escalates. Fear, either of doing well or of failing, paralyzes dialogue and process. Examples like this are numerous. We know the stories too well. We hear of them through colleagues who have stepped away from ministry or who are seriously considering doing so, and we know of them from weary congregations whose ministry has been derailed by the personal struggles of their pastors.

But we know there are also other stories and other examples. A relatively healthy, self-aware pastoral presence points a congregation to what is good and possible. Such pastoral guidance includes clarity of calling and purpose, the capacity to be appropriately connected and detached, a deep commitment to the work of ministry, interests and pursuits outside of ministry, and sustained integrity in the full array of circumstances in which ministers find themselves. Self-aware pastors are not as easily hooked by other people's issues; rather they are present and engaged with the members of the congregation, but they also maintain independent mood, thought, and spirit.

Pastoral presence of this kind creates an energizing openness and fosters an emotional well-being in the congregation. As a result, decisions can be made and enacted rather than just discussed. The calling of the church comes into clearer focus and translates into more specific priorities and strategies. People more often recognize and honor boundaries and participate in less role confusion. The congregation gains a greater sense of perspective about the urgency and importance of an issue. And

7. Online at www.lillyendowment.org/religion_ncr.html.

last but not least, emotionally unhealthy people are less able to hold congregations hostage to needs and whims that have little to do with the work of the church.[8]

Several interesting turning points occur in the story commonly known as the parable of the prodigal son.[9] Opportunities for identifying with someone in the story are rich and varied. These include the audacious request of the younger son to receive in advance his part of his father's inheritance, to the father barely letting the son finish an apology before calling for a celebration, to the older son's displeasure with the way his dad had handled the whole thing. Verse 17 begins with the conjunction "but," announcing perhaps the most important turn in the story. "But when he came to himself . . ."

The New International Version translates that verse as "When he came to his senses," and continues with a comparison between how well the hired hands were eating back home and how hungry the younger son was in this far off land. This calculation led him to make the only reasonable choice one could make in that situation, which was to go back home where there was more than enough food, even for the hired hands. In the NIV's wording it is clear that the younger son has recognized what would make the most practical sense in that situation. Practical wisdom is important, and even the New Revised Standard Version Bible (NRSV) makes it clear that the younger son was evaluating carefully what options would serve him best. But isn't something more conveyed in the NRSV's phrasing of the first part of verse 17? What does it mean that "he came to himself"? Is that not a way to describe how the younger son got out from underneath the expectations of others, some very unfortunate circumstances, and his self-inflicted burdens, and, at least for a moment, remembered his truest identity?

Your field education experience will be a grand success if it causes you to come to yourself, to know and appreciate and embrace who you are as a person created in the image of Love itself and valued infinitely by God. That is the first, truest thing that can be said about you and me. You and I are God's own, and God desires that we flourish—and that the whole creation flourishes—in abundant life. Powerfully authentic ministry flows from that flourishing.

8. More will be said about this in chapter 6. In addition, see Friedman, *Failure of Nerve*.

9. Luke 15:11–32, NIV.

WHEN MINISTRY GETS PERSONAL

Some seminary students are eager to begin field education because it represents their chance to learn and practice congregational leadership skills. Other students desire to gain pastoral experience, as well as to support a congregation through student ministry activities, but they do not look forward to the kind of introspection that most field education programs require. The reticence of these students often grows out of the awareness that doing ministry will activate issues that they would rather not face, much less discuss, with a supervisor and a group of peers. And yet, ministry is so personal that it is hard to imagine we can vibrantly engage its work if we do not deal honestly with the personal issues that might threaten the integrity and spirit of our ministry. When things from our past are left unattended, more often than not they will undermine pastoral presence and squelch pastoral voice.

You will be bumping into your life throughout your field education experience. Some of these moments will be exhilarating. For example, you may discover and be able to articulate for the first time what about the gospel really claims you and animates your ministry. You will remember those experiences as times when your call to ministry gained new clarity and energy. Other moments will leave you wondering what happened and usually a little embarrassed. Some experiences will trigger disproportionate and extraneous responses. As a result, the fear and pain that continue to linger in your life will take center stage, and ministry-related conversations might get derailed in the process.

For instance, you may be leading a meeting about a much needed and well-planned ministry initiative when someone redirects the conversation to last night's ball game. Your attempts to refocus the group go unheeded. The more you try to bring the conversation back the more the group talks about last night's game, then about other games this season, and finally about how this season compares with previous seasons. Your frustration comes to a boil, evidenced by your outburst: "This church is going to die if we cannot decide on some directions for our ministry and commit ourselves to them! We need to vote on this tonight so that we can get started."

Even if what you have said is true, you know that you have not handled that moment very well. Only in an extreme minority of situations, church or otherwise, does the entire future hinge on one conversation or one decision. Any number of things might be driving your overreaction and exaggeration, just as any number of things might have rerouted the group's attention away from your proposal and toward the ball game, but it is most obvious that the conversation has now shifted away from the ministry proposal and toward you and your uptightness. Moreover, it will take a while before this idea can be discussed again on its merits, in part because your anxiety has spilled over to the group.

Your eruption could have been driven by any number of issues. It is not always bad when your pain or fear become evident to those around you. In fact, there are occasions when your vulnerability invites others to explore and overcome their own pain and fear. Your focus should be on cultivating a deep and current self-awareness that allows you to be present in ways that can facilitate hope and healing in others. A lack of self-awareness, however, puts pastoral voice and its many possibilities for leadership always beyond reach.

A meeting like the one described above is just one example of where and how some tender places in the pastor's life might be revealed. Such tender issues also may surface when you lead worship, preach, teach, lead a small group, and care for those who are ill and struggling. You will be able to satisfactorily resolve some personal issues, and your ministry will genuinely grow out of a clearer understanding of your true self. You may work on other issues for a long time, much in the same way that living into your call to ministry is a lifelong process. You may never resolve other issues to your satisfaction, but having an awareness of them can at least help you foster a happier life and minimize the ways that your ministry is impeded by them.

In the previous chapter we discussed the importance of engaging a breadth of experience at your ministry site. Doing so causes you to become better acquainted and comfortable with the various roles and responsibilities of pastoral work. Along the way, you will begin to recognize the consistency and differences in your emerging voice from one area of ministry to another. A breadth of experience at your field education site also creates as many spaces for your personal issues to bubble up which, in turn, will lead you to greater self-understanding about who you are and what claims you and frightens you, both as a person and a minister.

Personal issues vary in nature and degree from person to person, of course, but the following list briefly describes some issues that seem to be particularly common among those preparing for ministry.

- A need for affirmation and approval. Some may be drawn to ministry because they perceive that it will afford them the recognition and reinforcement that they have not received anywhere else. For these people, the ministry is a platform that elevates them in the eyes of others; and in that elevated role these ministers experience the love and appreciation that, to that point in their lives, had not come their way. Most people in a congregation love, appreciate, and support their pastors, but that does not mean congregants wake up every morning thinking of ways to affirm their pastor. The congregation does not exist to prop up its pastor's emotional life.

- The habit of over-commitment. People-pleasers regularly over commit themselves in order to make sure everyone else is happy. Related to the first issue on this list, the desire to please other people compromises an individual's ministry in significant, even deadly, ways. Instead of holding fast to the priorities of pastoral work, over and over again these ministers try to meet real and manufactured needs of particular congregants at the expense of guiding congregational life. People-pleasing pastors usually find out that certain members of their congregations have a voracious appetite that never gets satisfied. Everyone ends up miserable, most of all the pastor, whose exhaustion and resentment grows out of his or her personal need to please others.

- Unclear boundaries. It naturally follows that people who crave affirmation and who willingly go to any extreme to please others will have boundary issues with their emotional spaces and personal time. In an effort to find pastoral voice, pastors must decide exactly where they end and other people begin. Healthy boundaries depend on saying yes and saying no, and then living by those commitments. For example, no one will believe that Friday is your Sabbath day until you believe it enough to practice it. Boundary-challenged pastors spend their days and nights reacting and, in the process, forfeit the chance to determine what will characterize their ministry.

- A lack of personal and pastoral clarity. Without rigorous reflection, people cannot discover their true selves. Although we can understand ourselves by way of the many roles we play in life, a lack of personal clarity leads an individual to capitulate to the expectations of others. The upshot to a lack of clarity around personal and pastoral identity is that it impedes the attempts of a congregation to arrive at its own theological and missional clarity.

- Conflict avoidance. If these preceding issues are present in a pastor, then a discomfort with conflict is almost sure to follow. Our dancing here and there to avoid conflict may prevent disagreement and discord in the short-term, but in the long run it frustrates others and undermines our ministry. Conflict is always present in human relations. Rather than run from conflict, pastors should think of it as a context for their ministry that is real, one that allows them to speak to things that matter. The amount of willful engagement with conflict reveals the extent to which pastors have gotten over their infatuation with being pastors, and demonstrates the level to which they can practice their personal convictions about ministry and faith.

- Anxiety plagues many people. In addition to personal sources of anxiety, many aspects of American culture cultivate anxiety. Being anxious does not rule out being a pastor, but you do need to discover what triggers your anxiety and how you can manage it. We all carry some levels of anxiety—it is a result of the finiteness of being human. Effective pastoral leadership calls for a nonreactive presence that refuses to shoulder the anxiety of a troubled congregational system. Individuals who are riddled with anxiety will find that being a nonreactive presence is a difficult task, so difficult that professional help may be required to help them effectively address their anxieties.

- Depression. Unfortunately, this condition is rather common among ministers. For the purposes of this discussion, it is sufficient to say that depression is a complex experience that calls for sensitivity, attention, professional diagnosis, and customized treatment. Its presentation varies from person to person, but people who experience depression frequently have symptoms that include indifference, withdrawal, and a lack of energy. In addition to the personal anguish, any level of depression makes it exceedingly difficult for a person to engage consistently the demands of ministry with stamina, enthusiasm, and purpose.

- Unresolved grief. This grief may extend well into the past, or it may be related to more recent losses. Wherever grief dwells, and whatever its nature and qualities, the pressures of ministry will likely bring any unresolved grief to the forefront. For example, as exciting as coming to seminary might be for students on one level, it is nonetheless probably a decision that has caused people some losses. Perhaps some gave up a successful and financially lucrative career, and so maybe they have forgone professional status or prestige. Perhaps some are attending seminary against the express wishes of an authority figure in their life, and in doing so have lost a valued aspect of their personal life. In addition to carrying heavy grief from prior endings, beginning something new will be emotionally hard.

These issues and other obstacles can severely diminish and compromise a minister and his or her work. Moreover, these issues can combine to create a troubling downward spiral. It is understandable that a person might wish to disengage from these personal issues, for denial provides an easy short-term solution. Exploring methods to overcome deep personal issues is beyond the scope of this book. But we can consider simplified forms of such methods. For example, Laraine Herring speaks to this issue in terms of writer's block. She contends that the only way for something to emerge from a moment of writer's block is to keep showing up and staying with the discomfort and uncertainty.[10] The more deeply we go into our own lives, the more understandable and manageable any threatening blocks will become. As a result, our words and witness will be more authentically compelling.

Looked at in this light, the question then is not just what we must personally activate by engaging in ministry, but what we must do about the things we activate. In supervised ministry, teachers employ various approaches to help students think about the work they need to do. Some of these approaches produce greater awareness through relatively simple methods of self-discovery. Others are far more complex and involved. What follows is a brief description of five of those approaches, beginning with the least complex.

First, students in supervised ministry often write case studies. These are one to two page descriptions of a recent event from the student's ministry that they then discuss in a small peer group. Practical wisdom usually surfaces about how to handle a particular situation or challenge, but the discussion focuses mostly on helping the students understand their

10. Herring, *Writing Begins with the Breath*, 50.

part in what transpired, what hooked them in that ministry event, and what future steps might be called for as they continue to explore this issue.

Second, field education provides numerous opportunities for students to understand their tendencies when dealing with conflict. A particularly helpful book for this discovery is Speed B. Leas's *Discover Your Conflict Management Style.*[11] A survey in that book helps students recognize their individual preferred conflict management style (persuading, compelling, avoiding/accommodating, collaborating, negotiating, and supporting), identify the strengths and vulnerabilities of each style, and understand ways to lead with their nonpreferred conflict management styles when situations call for that. The conversation also presses students to think about why they are more comfortable with one style than the others. Very often, a direct line can be traced to how conflict was handled in the family of origin.

Third, the Myers-Briggs Type Indicator (MBTI), which dates to the 1940s, poses a series of questions designed to reveal personality types. The MBTI is not without its critics. I offer it here not because I think being a "J" or an "I" (MBTI lettering for judging and introversion, respectively) captures the complexity of any human life. It does not. However, within its limitations, the MBTI makes two contributions. First, it can lead students to further self-understanding by identifying personality types and the tendencies of those types. Second, certain personality types pose particular challenges and pitfalls to clergy. The book *Personality Type and Religious Leadership* by Oswald and Kroeger is especially helpful in identifying both the strengths and vulnerabilities that accompany various personality types.[12]

Fourth, creating a personal timeline can help students understand their particular journey and how their call to ministry grows out of that journey. Some versions of this exercise require students to use a series of post-it notes to construct a personal thick description, in which students describe in some detail the pivotal moments and life events that have sent their lives in a particular direction and profoundly shaped their understanding of themselves. Students identify on a separate post-it note each person, place, event, and circumstance that has shaped and influenced them. One color of post-it notes is used for positive experiences; another

11. Leas, *Discover Your Conflict Management Style.*

12. Oswald and Kroeger, *Pesonality Type and Religious Leadership*, 124–35.

color for negative ones. The next step is to look for natural groupings of these experiences, either by themes, seasons, or transitions. Once grouped, students identify things they have learned from each of these groupings. As one student put it, "I would have never thought about some of this garbage in my life if I had not been required to do so for this assignment."

Fifth, some issues can only be worked through sufficiently in therapy. As Laraine Herring says, one of the first tasks of writing is to open up the energy center so that you can access your voice.[13] Therapy helps a person to do that, but ministers are notoriously bad about asking for help. Those people who meet with a therapist regularly often describe it as life-giving. For them, therapy ensures that issues do not accumulate and go unattended. Frederick Buechner writes, "It is important to tell at least from time to time the secret of who we truly and fully are. Otherwise we run the risk of losing track of who we truly and fully are and come to accept instead the highly edited version which we put forth in the hope that the world will find it more appealing than the real thing."[14]

These and other resources help students find pastoral voice; likewise they can help pastors stay current in their relationships with others and with themselves. These activities are designed to help you foster an inner life that is able to support your outer life of public ministry. Your pastoral voice emerges when you sort and prioritize the issues in your life. You will want to claim some of these issues. Others you will want to lay to rest. This kind of introspection will lead you to a heightened capacity for renewed self-awareness and honest self-assessment, which in turn frees you to express your deepest hope through your ministry.

HOW SELF-UNDERSTANDING GIVES RISE TO PASTORAL VOICE: SOME CASE STUDIES

The two case studies below show how personal issues can enhance or hinder the development and exercise of pastoral voice.

13. Herring, *Writing Begins with the Breath*, 25.
14. Buechner, *Telling Secrets*, 3.

When Esther Met Marcus

Esther, the longtime treasurer at Prince of Peace Church, made an appointment with Pastor Marcus, saying she wanted to brief Marcus about the church's financial statements in advance of an upcoming church council meeting. Marcus had become the pastor at Prince of Peace only three months prior, and this would be his first council meeting.

As it turned out, Esther's trip to the church that day was more about recruiting than briefing. She believed that those who were accountable for the finances at Prince of Peace kept poor records, ignored the system of checks and balances that were in place, and regularly committed funds that the church did not have for projects. Esther had been trying for years, unsuccessfully, to change the budgeting and spending practices at Prince of Peace. By contrast, nobody else seemed overly concerned about these practices. Most of the congregational leaders thought of Esther as an alarmist. It frustrated her terribly that no one else was as anxious as she was about this matter.

Fortunately for Esther, Marcus was new to the place. He was eager to listen to her, to learn about the congregation, and to do well in his ministry. Perhaps he was too eager. Esther blew into his office with all kinds of charts, graphs, and anecdotes, all of which pointed to a financial crisis for the congregation. She repeated statistics, account balances, and stories, each time scooting her chair a little closer to where Marcus sat. Every round of reports created more gloom. "You see why I am concerned, don't you, pastor?"

The pastor's reply at first was vague and noncommittal. "This is a lot of information. You think a lot about this, don't you?" Those comments were sincere and straightforward. They seemed to put the ball back in Esther's court, but for some reason Marcus did not stop there. "The church is lucky to have someone like you who pays so much attention to its finances." Marcus wondered immediately why he had said that. He really did not know whether Esther was a good church treasurer or if the church was lucky or not. Church finances energized Esther tremendously for some reason, but his conversation-shifting comment would probably keep him from finding out why. Marcus had given just what Esther had sought, an opening to cultivate an ally and to leverage sympathy.

Esther quickly sensed the weak spot and moved to exploit it. "That's very kind of you, pastor. I just want to support my church and this is one way I can do that. I think we were lucky to get you, especially with your background. The council will want to know your initial impressions of our church and I can't think of any situations that are more critical than our finances."

By the time Esther left, Marcus was a hapless pile of compliance. She had observed Marcus in his first few weeks at the church. She knew Marcus could be manipulated, and on this visit she had pushed all the right, or wrong, buttons. For all his gifts for ministry, Marcus struggled mightily with three issues. First, he had a deep need to be liked. He was not going to challenge or disagree with Esther. He was concerned that if he challenged Esther, then she would not to like him. And that, in turn, would jeopardize the relationship he needed to have with Esther in order for his ministry to flourish.

Second, Marcus had never become comfortable with other people's pain. In fact, he was so uncomfortable with it that he gladly absorbed it into himself. After situations like this he often became angry and disappointed with himself when he realized what he had done; but in the moment his first inclination usually was to do whatever was necessary to ease someone else's pain or concern. In this case, he relieved Esther of all her anxiety (though she undoubtedly soon found other reasons to be anxious) and allowed it to rest squarely and literally upon his shoulders. Tense neck muscles provided the first clue that he had fallen for Esther's ploy.

Third, Marcus enjoyed stepping in and saving situations that he felt, without his help, would otherwise doom its victims to certain ruin and demise. This messiah complex and inflated sense of self (or was it a deflated sense of self?) resulted in Marcus rather frequently exaggerating both the direness of a situation and the positive results of his efforts. Marcus had a way of referring to his arrival at that congregation as if it coincided with the beginning of time itself. This annoyed quite a few people, of course, but many found some perverse satisfaction in Marcus's need to be needed.

Esther manipulated Marcus in that first meeting and on a few subsequent occasions. A group of Esther's friends realized they could fairly easily recruit Marcus to side with them on issues that were important to them. Within a year Marcus had allowed himself and his ministry to be compromised. Prior to ministry, he had dealt with similar situations by leaving—jobs, relationships, and locales. This time, however, he chose to stay and work through some issues that had plagued him since middle school. Marcus's strong sense of call motivated him to delve more deeply into his past. He wanted to be an effective pastor and knew that would always be beyond his reach unless he worked on his own life first. A therapist helped him see how his parents' divorce at that time either caused or exacerbated an insecurity that left him badly needing to be liked and terribly uncomfortable with conflict. During his middle school years, he had attempted to rescue his parents and their marriage. At fourteen, he developed a pattern of absorbing the pain of people around him.

Fortunately, at the age of thirty-six, he entered therapy. Over the next few years, Marcus became aware of how other incidents and issues had shaped his personality. His therapy caused him to confront many painful moments, and again his first inclination was to run. Instead he pushed through those times for the sake of his own well-being.

Marcus served as pastor of Prince of Peace Church for twelve years. Of the many beneficial things that occurred during that time, two are worth noting here. First, the more Marcus focused on his emotional and spiritual well-being, the more discerning and engaging the congregation became in its life and worship. Second, Esther resigned as church treasurer about halfway through Marcus's tenure and became considerably less active in the congregation. Once Marcus developed more clarity about his life, and the congregation began exhibiting a commitment to its own healthy processes, Esther started spending a lot of time at the town library, where she already had convinced the director that the library's finances were a total mess.

Reia's Righteous Indignation

Reia came to seminary to prepare for ministry, even though she had no church home, no sponsoring congregation, and no denominational endorsement. Some believed Reia left the church of her childhood and early adulthood, but she contended that it is the other way around. The church left her, and a whole host of other people, when it took a sharp theological and political turn.

Reia grew up in Charles Street Baptist Church, a large Southern Baptist Church near Atlanta where both of her parents joined the staff in 1984. The church featured great music and preaching, encouraged individual autonomy on matters of belief, and continually launched community ministries that benefitted various marginalized groups in the city. Even though a Fundamentalist element in the Southern Baptist Convention had been steering the Convention away from its historic commitments, not to mention gutting some top flight colleges and seminaries of academic freedom and integrity, during the first half of the 1990s Charles Street had been able to withstand the attacks and manipulation from these forces of change. However, when the senior pastor retired in 1995, Convention Fundamentalists in the area saw it as a chance they had been waiting on for nearly twenty years.

Fundamentalist leaders knew from previous campaigns that they would find members at Charles Street who were sympathetic to their cause. Even though Charles Street had aligned itself with the moderate stream of Southern Baptists, in the past numerous members had contributed financially to help build a Fundamentalist network that stretched from Virginia through Texas. Fundamentalist leaders in the area started attending worship services, Bible studies, and small groups at Charles Street.

Reia concedes that she probably tells a slanted version of the story, but the personal nature of what occurred there makes objectivity nearly impossible. The first person fired was a close friend of Reia's parents, a woman in her forties who had guided the congregation through several staff transitions and two building projects in her role as church administrator. Reia's mother, who was the longtime and immensely popular director of small groups, was the second person terminated. The same group of deacons who had supported these two women enthusiastically and given them several increases in pay and benefits suddenly determined that it was inappropriate for women to fill these two key roles. In addition to essentially functioning as part of the pastoral staff, these two women also were supervising men. With their newfound biblical interpretation, these deacons could not tolerate women in positions of authority.

Reia's dad, who as minister of evangelism was widely credited with Charles Street's unparalleled, decade-long, numerical growth, resigned in protest two months later when it was clear that no amount of appeal would change things. With little severance and less explanation, Reia and her parents quickly had to find a way to support themselves until another call came. When money ran out, the family moved in with Reia's maternal grandparents. While living there, all three of them shared a bedroom.

They stayed busy looking for new ministry positions, as well as for secular employment. Two years later, just as Reia was entering college, her parents accepted a co-pastorate at a church in a neighboring state. While they continue to serve that congregation, a measure of distrust and suspicion understandably lingers from what they experienced years ago at Charles Street.

For Reia, many issues and questions surfaced during this wilderness experience. She alternated between raging anger and debilitating depression. In the early years, Reia directed most of her anger toward the Charles Street congregation for obvious reasons, but she soon realized that her parents' decision to remain in ministry and then serve at another church also infuriated her. She felt as betrayed by her parents as she did by her former church. Some of this, she would later discover, had to do with some parent-child issues that had gone unresolved from her teenage years. Still other aspects of this anger grew out of some serious challenges she was dealing with while she attended high school.

In addition to issues that cried out for support and healing, Reia recognized some possibilities while in that wilderness. She knew others had lost their theological home and that the church had betrayed their trust. She wondered how many of them were clergy or came from clergy families. Reia wanted to know where people turned when they had been cast out from that place in which they had invested much of their lives.

Reia looked for a support group designed especially for people in her situation but could not find one. She found a grief support group that was sponsored by a local hospice affiliate and joined it. Some people in the group were grieving the death of family members, but several others were working through loss of other kinds. Reia found friendship and healing through this group. She also discerned a calling.

A year later, Reia enrolled in a dual-degree program at a seminary where she would earn a master of divinity degree and a master's degree in psychotherapy and faith. The latter course work involved additional therapy, which she welcomed. Following seminary, she accepted a chaplaincy position at a local hospital and found fulfillment in that ministry, but she continued to look for ways to provide support and hope to clergy and clergy families who might be reeling from painful situations in the church.

In 2011, Reia joined the staff of an urban counseling center that offers a wide array of services. With significantly reduced fees for clergy, it attracts numerous area pastors and ministers. In some ways, this is a dream come true for Reia. She loves working with people who find themselves in situations that are at least as difficult as Reia and her parents found themselves in so many years ago. And yet, all these years later, Reia often finds herself hooked by a story of a pastor or a pastor's spouse or child. Without constant attention, she can inaccurately extrapolate someone else's details into a narrative that looks exactly like her own. She continues to work with her supervising therapist about how best to serve clergy clients in light of this issue. From time to time, Reia thinks about attending a worship service at a local church, but she has not done so yet.

CULTIVATING VOICE: GIVING OURSELVES TO MINISTRY

When I was a pastor working with couples who were preparing for marriage, I would ask each person in a couple to create two timelines. I asked them to complete the first timeline and then meet with me in a follow-up session. Then, after that session, I would ask them to create the second timeline. I instructed each person to complete his or her timeline independently and not share it with his or her partner until the follow-up session.

The first timeline was a personal record of the past. I asked each person to chart his or her life to that point, from birth to the present moment, and identify noteworthy people, events, circumstances, joys, and disappointments along the way. I learned that many people came to the follow-up meeting expecting to tell about their own timeline, which would have had its own benefit. But they were invariably surprised when instead I asked each person to tell about the other's timeline. The prospective groom would try his best to describe his fiancée's timeline, and vice versa. When the groom, for example, had named everything he thought might be on his fiancée's timeline, the bride would have the chance to mention things that had not come up yet. Sometimes the conversations held major surprises. In one session, a man blurted out at his wife-to-be, "What? You lived in Korea for three years!" I wondered if they had ever talked with each other during their fifteen-month courtship.

The second timeline, also completed independently and kept in confidence until a later session, began with their wedding day and extended as far into the future as they wanted to take it. Again, they did not share their own anticipated story in the follow-up session but, again, attempted to describe what their partner's future timeline looked like. This timeline was designed to help them see the extent to which their ideas and plans coincided or conflicted. Part of the conversation also allowed them to identify—usually with some prompting—how realistic some of their projections were, what concessions they were already making, and how they felt about some of those compromises. This put conflicts and limits on the table that they had overlooked or even denied in their excitement about getting married. In one instance, the prospective groom's timeline included medical school and a stint in Africa with Doctors without Borders. The prospective bride's future story acknowledged medical school as a necessary stepping stone, but clearly looked forward to a life supported by a very lucrative specialty practice in the suburbs. (The good news is that they are still married to each other all these years later.)

Following this two-part exercise, I asked each person to find connections between the two timelines. For example, I would ask each person, "What is consistent between the life you describe in your first timeline and the life you describe in your second one? What from your own values, priorities, and dreams connect the two? Are you able to see the truest expression of yourself in both of these timelines?" On more than one occasion, it seemed that one or both persons had very quickly lost themselves during their courtship. They had become so enmeshed in the relationship that their individually distinctive identities had faded. The revealing of this truth can pose a far greater threat to the future of a relationship than not knowing your partner lived in Korea for three years or that he intends to spend three years in Africa.

Consider using these two timelines to help you think about your journey in ministry. Let's say that your first timeline begins with your birth and extends through seminary graduation. The second timeline begins with your first call after seminary and stretches as far into the future as you wish. I frequently hear ministers describe a disturbing disconnect between these two parts of their lives. Often, it seems that pastors have lost touch with the hope, passion, and interests that characterized their earlier lives. They appear unable to access that which caused them to pursue ministry in the first place. A common lament is, "I think I would be a better Christian if I were not a pastor." The specific meaning of such a statement varies from minister to minister. In some cases, ministers need to step back and become better acquainted with what it first means to be a disciple, a follower of Jesus. In other cases, it may reveal that the minister has allowed the realities of pastoral life and work to get in the way of what, in previous days or years, stirred his or her heart and mind. If that is the case, it is little wonder that many find ministry so unfulfilling. Distance has crept in between who the person is and the ministry that is being attempted.

The apostle Paul founded the church in Thessalonica and later wrote to the Christians there to encourage them, as well as to defend himself against accusations concerning his character and motives. While with the Thessalonians, Paul says that he and his friends not only were focused on sharing the gospel of God, but "also our own selves."[15] Ministry in this case grew out of the lives of those offering the ministry.

The Thessalonians are dear to Paul, and he uses tender yet powerful language to care for them "like a nurse tenderly caring for her own children."[16] Even though Paul and his friends had been shamefully mistreated and had encountered strong opposition on several occasions, they did not seek praise or gain or leverage. Instead, they cared for the Christians there so deeply that they shared their own selves.

Paul, of course, was not the only biblical figure to use the imagery of nursing. Many biblical passages employ it as a metaphor for God's comfort and faithfulness.[17] Indeed, few things express more intimacy than nursing a child. As a male, I am exceedingly hesitant to tread on this sacred ground, but Paul's use of nursing as a metaphor for ministry is too compelling to resist. Nursing is a far more pleasant experience, I am told, when both the mother and the child are calm and at ease. When the nursing mother is stressed and anxious—an understandable state of being given the circumstances—such a state often inhibits the milk letdown and can even diminish the milk supply.

In ministry, stress and anxiety inhibit the flow of the abundance from our hearts. Tension over unfinished business and unresolved issues drives a wedge between who we are as individuals and the ministry we want to offer. When we do not deal with matters from our past, whether we are talking two decades or two hours ago, those matters will distort our faith

15. 1 Thess 2:8.
16. 1 Thess 2:7.
17. See Isa 49:15 and 66:11–13.

and undermine our ministry. Paul speaks of being gentle, but we cannot truly be gentle with others unless we are also gentle toward ourselves. Ministry involves vulnerability, and lingering guilt and doubt builds walls that neither let others in nor ourselves out. On the other hand, when we stay current with what is going on in our lives and do not allow pent up emotions to accumulate, we are freer to give ourselves, our truest selves, in an encouraging and hopeful ministry.

At some point you likely will have the chance to help write a congregational future story with a church you will be serving, but for now think about your personal future story.

- What will your second timeline, the one that begins with your first call after seminary, look like?

- What personal experiences will shape the tone and priorities of your ministry?

- What of your own values will get expressed through your ministry?

- In what ways will your faith and spirituality overflow into your ministry?

- How will the spirit of healing that you have known in your own life be contagiously evident in your ministry?

- How will your understanding of what it means to be a Christian dictate how you spend your time as a pastor?

- What is your deepest hope as an individual, and how will that hope impact those with whom you will live and serve in the church and the wider community?

- How will you stay in touch with what enlivens, energizes, and renews you?

Now, while you are preparing for ministry, is the time to commit yourself to approaching the end of your ministry, whether that is ten years away or forty, with grace and vitality. Ministers who finish well maintain healthy patterns throughout the seasons. Those who try to make up in their last two years for thirty years of imbalance and bad habits usually find there is too much to overcome.

Your future story as a minister of the gospel will be about more than simply leading a successively larger series of congregations. Rather, your ministry should plunge you into what animates your life and, upon coming back up, ask you to translate those things into specific strategies and concrete actions that then constitute your ministry. So what stirs your soul? What makes your heart sing?

For example, at an ordination service one of the ministers gave the following charge to the candidate, just before she kneeled for the laying on of hands. "You, Shekala, have an extraordinary belly laugh. It expresses something wonderful and deep about you as a person and a minister. It has reverberated around the halls of this seminary for three years and I have no doubt it has filled all the spaces where you have ever been. If it ever goes away, if it ever diminishes, if it is at any point no longer heard in the rooms of your home and the hallways of the congregation where you serve, then something has happened at your core and it is time to investigate what has changed and find ways to address it."

Of all the beautiful, hopeful words spoken and sung at that ordination service, those are the ones I remember. They resonated with many who were sitting near me. If something that expresses your truest self ever goes away or diminishes for very long at all, it is time to investigate. Something has changed about you and, for your sake and those around you, before too much of what gives you life starts to drain away, you need to see what has changed and then address it. Otherwise, the essence of who you are will become foreign to you and your ministry.

Who are you at your center, and how will that identity be evident in your ministry? Creative? Hospitable? Curious? Compassionate? Courageous? Imaginative? Spiritually alive? Physically active? Interested and interesting?

And how will those facets of you play out in your ministry? As a sympathetic companion, or a supportive friend, or a risk-taker, or a calming presence, or a disciplined leader, or a gracious facilitator?

These aspects of you are not manufactured for an occasional theme or a special emphasis, but rather are the overflow of your life. They spring from what matters most deeply to you and are woven into everything you are and do. As Laraine Herring says of those who have lost sight of themselves as writers, "They hadn't maintained and nurtured a relationship with their writing over the years, so it had, quite simply, quit waiting around for them to show up."[18] But, to paraphrase Howard Thurman, those who maintain and nurture that relationship between the person

18. Herring, *Writing Begins with the Breath*, 53.

and the pastor, who are always learning about themselves and their ministry, speak to their time with their very lives.[19]

---

19. Fluker and Tumber, *Strange Freedom*, 261.

6

Finding Your Place in the System

The author is not only himself but his predecessors, and simultaneously he is part of the living tribal fabric, the part that voices what we all know, or should know, and need to hear.[1]

—John Updike

A GROUP WITH A LIFE OF ITS OWN

The previous chapter provided you ways to think about the hopes, joys, fears, and wounds that are a part of your life. Aware of them or not, working through them or not, you will take them with you everywhere you go, including on your journey of ministry. They will be with you as you attempt to exegete a context, interpret the Christian story, and fulfill pastoral roles for a congregation. Sometimes they will enhance your work and sometimes they will undermine it.

Few, if any, of your joys and wounds developed in a vacuum. You did not learn to trust or distrust other people, for instance, in isolation. You learned through direct encounters with others. Many of these encounters occurred while you were a member of a group, formal or informal, beginning with your family and continuing on into your social, educational, work, and recreational interactions. Not only did you find hope or harm

1. Shaughnessy, *Walking on Alligators*, 14.

in your experiences with those clusters of people, but you also took on a certain identity and played a particular role within each. Moreover, the groups at home, school, work, and play often functioned in predictable patterns and abided by unwritten rules and norms that were more or less clear. And because you moved in and out of various groups in the course of a week, you may have played different roles in different groups. All of these groups function as systems, and the power and influence can be felt long after they have dissolved or when we no longer regularly participate in them. For example, we may move out of our parents' house when we are eighteen, but the dynamics in our family of origin will stay with us as long as we live.

You will spend your ministry in some type of a system. Some seminary students shy away from congregational ministry because they do not want to become entangled in the messy politics and organizational machinery of such work. But if you become a chaplain in a hospital, you will find yourself within a rather complicated system. And if you become a chaplain in the military, you may discover yourself to be a member of a miniscule part in an immensely convoluted system. Indeed, usually one unit of Clinical Pastoral Education is enough for students to understand that institutional chaplaincy involves its own channels, conflicts, and concessions. Some of the dynamics between congregational ministry and institutional chaplaincy will differ and some will be similar. Regardless, ministry occurs within systems.

Systems theory[2] is a common way to think about congregational life and group dynamics. A congregation is a system, and in a congregational system every tentacle is on full alert, maintaining status quo, guarding against change and difference of opinion, looking for an issue to exploit, and bending each new person into compliance with the assumptions and perceptions of that system. Pastors often give remarkable care and attention to people in one-to-one settings, but even the most capable pastors can get caught completely off guard by systemic dynamics that swirl around them. The most inwardly turned systems can cause otherwise

---

2. For a more thorough examination of systems theory, especially in regard to the interrelatedness between the congregation, the family of origin, and the pastor and his or her family, see Edwin H. Friedman, *Generation to Generation: Family Process in Church and Synagogue.* For a concise treatment of how congregations function from a systems perspective, see Peter L. Steinke, *How Your Church Family Works: Understanding Congregations as Emotional Systems* and *Congregational Leadership for Anxious Times: Being Calm and Courageous No Matter What.*

high functioning, independent-thinking people to submit to a group's anxiety and behavior. Needy, immature, imprecise pastors typically struggle in congregational systems in two ways—either they overcompensate for their neediness and lack of clarity with a shrill, overreaching pastoral voice that attempts to manipulate everything and everybody, or they completely forfeit themselves and their identity and, as a result, take every cue from a system that simply wants to be pain free and unchanged.

When seeking to claim and cultivate your pastoral voice, there are four aspects of systemic thinking that you should carefully consider.

First, in systems thinking, a group focuses on the whole and the interrelatedness of its parts rather than on its individual parts. In congregations, an action by any one part impacts every other part. It is impossible to make only one change. A change with one person affects every person, and a change with a subgroup in the congregation affects every other subgroup.

Congregational systems, especially, prefer to isolate problem parts. This isolation occurs when someone acts out or does not properly perform a function. Systems like to break things down and find somebody to blame. If, for example, the worship team leader is not showing up for worship, not calling meetings in order to plan and prepare for worship, and not following through on assigned tasks, the system will find fault with the worship team leader. Case closed; no further discussion. Perhaps this is a case of personal irresponsibility. If so, that raises one set of questions about why this system put an irresponsible person into such an important position. We might also ask what is going on in the rest of this person's life, that is, in the other systems of which she is a part—family, friends, work, and other groups in the church. Is something afoot in one of those areas that is hampering her ministry in the congregation? But from the perspective of systems thinking, what is more likely is that a gifted, capable worship team chairperson is meeting with systemic resistance at every turn. In other words, the same system that asked her to do this job is effectively making sure she cannot accomplish what the job entails.

Congregations rarely look at the whole because doing so means delving into the incredible complexity of human relations. It means examining every person's role in a breakdown, and not just the one person or area that group has already decided should carry the blame. A minister with a strong pastoral voice is able to bring up the questions that rarely get asked, such as, What is going on in the system that has contributed to this person's lack of performance? Did the congregation thoroughly prepare her for the work she was given? Was it clear where she could turn for support, clarification, and resources? Has the congregation set her up for failure by asking her to do things the congregation really does not want done? Is the worship team a place where anxiety lurks, or is this anxiety generated in another corner of congregational life? And if so, why has this anxiety gravitated toward the worship team leader? Does she regularly seek out and take on other people's discomfort, or has the congregation heaped this anxiety on her because it has identified her as a scapegoat? Diagnosing a situation like this involves numerous angles and dynamics, many of which will not be readily apparent or discussed openly. Changing a system is even more difficult. As we will discuss later in this chapter, the key is paying attention to your own self-definition and functioning when the congregational system gets stuck.

Second, life in any system revolves around two needs: individuality and togetherness. That is, individuals have the need to be separate and, they also need to identify with the group. Some pastors are so separate that they are aloof and unresponsive to the needs of the group. Others overconnect with their congregations to the point that their identity is solely defined by whatever small group they are with at the moment. The responsibility of defining your individual self while remaining connected to the group falls to you. In short, who are you as a person and a pastor, and what will characterize your life and ministry? Your self-definition will be influenced and will change from time to time, but vigilant self-differentiation remains your task. It is a difficult task given the kind of praise, criticism, and indifference that you, as a pastor, will receive. Taking a poll and capitulating to the preferred identity of the moment might sound easier in the short term, but in the long term such practices will debilitate both you and the congregation.

Let us pause for a moment to explore the notion of self-differentiation more deeply. The balance that a person must strike between separating from a group and connecting to it is called "self-differentiation." Victor Hunter calls it "holy distance" and "holy intimacy."[3] Your ability to self-differentiate is determined by your personality type and your overall spiritual and emotional health, both of which are discussed in chapter 5 of this book. For example, introverts and extroverts handle separating from a group and connecting to it in different ways. Another way of thinking

---

3. Hunter, *Desert Hearts and Healing Fountains*, 43.

about connecting and separating is captured by Bernard Loomer, who claims that size or stature is the most essential spiritual and theological virtue. Loomer describes the capacity of an individual to embrace as much of life as possible without being overwhelmed by it as being "the volume of life you can take into your being and still maintain your integrity and individuality, the intensity and variety of outlook you can entertain in the unity of your being without feeling defensive or insecure."[4] Loomer's description speaks to the capacity you have to love others and foster their well-being while remaining clear about what matters to you and how you can best express that spirit and those commitments through your living.

A herd mentality often creeps into systems in order to protect whiners and demonize dissenters. This is especially the case in anxious, rigid systems that cannot tolerate ambiguity and difference. Howard Thurman once said that we have made an idol of togetherness,[5] and rarely is that more true than in a congregation that is huddled together in an attempt to keep the new and the true at bay. Systems bounded by an extreme togetherness will only welcome and absorb those people who will perpetuate the herd mentality and the fears and falsehoods upon which the group's continuance depends. When the whole system buys into fear and inflexibility, people often attempt to exploit a triangular relationship whereby they leverage one person against another person, idea, or circumstance. Even in congregations not bound by extreme togetherness, pastors will be a part of numerous triangles. It is simply a facet of congregational life. The key for pastors is to maintain a healthy self-differentiation, and in so doing minimize the times and degrees to which they become triangulated by another person for the sake of an argument or position they do not hold. Pastoral voice arises in relationship with other people, but it is not thoroughly dictated by other people.

Third, all relationship systems take on anxiety. In congregations where individual difference is valued and conflict is understood to be just one aspect of group dynamics, anxiety can translate into productive energy. Members of such a congregation may hear the sounds of anxiety to be a call to opportunity and adventure. By contrast, chronically timid and stuck congregations are acutely sensitive to the same sounds and usually interpret the noise of any upcoming change as a signal that

---

4. Loomer, "S-I-Z-E Is the Measure," 70.

5. Smith, *Howard Thurman: Essential Writings*, 150.

the congregation will soon experience a serious threat or another loss. Such congregations may never consider any other interpretations. Thus, instead of exploring what might be a fascinating ministry opportunity, their low threshold for pain and inconvenience causes them to retreat. Indeed, anxiety further narrows their vision of what is possible and cruelly diminishes their imagination. In some congregations, a proposed change triggers anxiety that is sourced from years and decades in the past. This anxiety may not be directly related to what is being discussed at the time, of course, and so a misdirected and disproportionate overreaction paralyzes the whole system.

Consider how many systems you are a part of and their interlocking nature; you can discover the potential emotional influences they have on each other. As Friedman notes, pastors are consistently involved in three distinctive family systems: the congregation as one family, the many families that make up the congregation, and the pastor's family. Unresolved anxiety in one relationship plays out in another one.[6] For example, unbridled anxiety in the pastor's family will take root in the congregation. Likewise, unchecked anxiety of a congregation's individual family will have the same affect. Conversely, chronic or acute anxiety in the congregation can spill over into the pastor's family and the other families in the congregation. It is also true that increased effectiveness in any one of these systems generates a positive impact on the others.

Systems thinking speaks of the importance of a nonanxious leader. However, I have never heard of anyone who is utterly without anxiety. We all carry some anxiety as a result of the finiteness of being human. A more realistic leadership trait is that of being a nonreactive presence in the midst of a disturbed congregational system that badly wants its leader to shoulder the group's anxiety. Ministers riddled with anxiety likely will find that being a nonreactive presence is quite a difficult task and may discover they need a wide range of professional help to maintain their own well-being and, in turn, the well-being of their ministry.

Fourth, systems, including congregations, seek homeostasis. In an effort to help a system achieve a state of relative balance, effective leaders try to understand what that system craves and what it dislikes. Ministers who have attempted change in their church for the sake of greater faithfulness have probably become well acquainted with the fierce tenacity with

---

6. Friedman, *Generation to Generation*, 1.

which a congregation grips the status quo. Tenacity brings to mind images of people engaged in intense battle in order to keep things the same. But tenacity has less warlike attributes that can prevent change nonetheless. Ronald Heifetz captures tenacity's softer powers when he speaks of the elegance of the status quo.[7] Numerous congregations move about their business with exquisite polish and appropriate protocol. The way they resist the new is to be unusually accomplished at what no longer works. Comfortable, elegant, stuck systems hate conflict and suppress it at every turn. When things run so smoothly, they reason, what could be wrong?

Systems theory argues against the common claim that pastors need more expertise to overcome resistance to the new. Instead, this theory focuses on increasing the pastor's capacity for separation and connection, which then leads to increased self-differentiation and higher functioning.[8] In addition to the congregation as a whole functioning at a higher level, the self-differentiation of the pastor will foster independence, clarity, and creativity among the congregants. Unfortunately, too often pastors, appropriately concerned about staying employed, believe that "getting along" is the most important thing that pastors and congregations can do. In those settings, pastors have no sense of agency. They lack independent thought and spirit. As a result, the whole enterprise of being church is held captive, unwilling to explore a more fulfilling, exciting life together. To challenge the church's captivity, some exceptionally well-differentiated people must step forward and embody that fulfilling, exciting venture of faith. Behold: the calling of ministry.

Steinke uses the three parts of the brain—the reptilian, the mammalian, and the neocortex—as an analogy for leadership in a congregational system.[9] The reptilian brain is reactive, instinctive, defensive, and intensely concerned about survival and self-preservation. The mammalian part of the brain focuses on bonding and playing, though it can be reactive as well. The neocortex is the thinking, planning, problem-solving, imagining part of the brain. The reptilian and the mammalian parts comprise only 15 percent of the brain, while the neocortex makes up 85 percent of it.

Now think about the congregations in which you have participated and served. In what part of the brain do they function most of the time?

7. Heifetz et al, *Practice of Adaptive Leadership*, 49.

8. Friedman, *Generation to Generation*, 2.

9. Steinke, *Congregational Leadership in Anxious Times*, 49–64.

Congregations need a reptilian brain because crises do arise, but some churches act exclusively from this perspective. They see threats everywhere, and they look and turn inwardly for the sake of their own exaggerated sense of survival. Congregations also depend on their mammalian brains to nurture fellowship and community, but they can go overboard and allow togetherness to distort their life and work. Many congregations are adept at using this 15 percent of the brain, while they rarely use their collective neocortex—the remaining 85 percent.

Leadership in a congregational system is the act of functioning as the neocortex for a community, and then fostering that capacity among the congregants. When the pastor understands and connects with the system, consistently practices self-differentiation, and regularly processes anxiety, she positions herself in a place to effectively say what the congregation perhaps already knows but needs to hear again. Her leadership will not necessarily lead her congregation to create smoother channels and deliver quicker answers. Instead, she will create an environment in which possibilities can be considered thoughtfully, costs can be fairly assessed, conflicts can be channeled toward productive energy, and the presence and purposes of God can be at the heart of the congregation. In those moments, what a congregation experiences is the elegance and the tenacity of pastoral voice.

UNDERSTANDING THE LIFE OF YOUR CONGREGATION

Many books have been written about congregational dynamics.[10] Although these resources have contributed greatly to our understanding of congregational dynamics, congregations nonetheless can make decisions and approach their life together in ways that will baffle even the most studied ministers, just as you will do some things that will baffle your congregation. Simply, congregations are full of people. And people, despite their accomplishments, talents, and good intentions have the capacity to think and act in strange and puzzling ways.

God be praised, sometimes the seemingly illogical and circuitous processes of making group decisions lead to life-giving, community-blessing ministry. The wind blows where it will, and those individuals

---

10. I especially recommend Israel Galindo, *The Hidden Lives of Congregations* for the discussion about the dynamics of size, life cycle, spirituality, and identity.

who are willing and able to position their sails to the Spirit's leading then find themselves on open-ended, unmarked, fulfilling adventures in ministry. Their orientation is outward, toward the immediate community and rest of the world, and their posture is born of mission. They seek God's presence and pursue possibilities that are in line with God's desired healing for the world. Some paths are cul-de-sacs that may reveal something important to these intrepid travelers, which leaves them richer for the experience as they then circle back out and embark on yet another course. Occasionally, these travelers are frustrated with outdated road signs, poorly marked trails, and impatient companions; but a truly robust congregational system supports and sustains them so that they may persevere in ways that are creative, truthful, and faithful.

On the other hand, God have mercy, some congregations meander interminably in discernment and discussion. At some point they entered a recognizable organizational cul-de-sac, perhaps even one that carried prominence in another era, and they took shelter there. The pace in such familiar surroundings is placid, the risks are minimal, and practically nothing will be asked or expected of them as individuals or as a church. These congregations refuse the call to adventure, no matter how many times their GPS (Global Positioning Spirit) announces "Recalculating."They will occasionally venture out of their home in the cul-de-sac, but will usually retreat fairly quickly upon realizing how much has changed in the outside world, and how much learning will be required of them in order to navigate the new traffic patterns. Overwhelmed, such congregations invariably focus their efforts inward. They pour over easily resolved matters and continue the same conversations month after month, year after year. These conversations are respectful and even pleasant, but often fall into "idolatrous togetherness."[11]

The two preceding descriptions capture congregational dynamics at their extremes. Indeed, in the real world, some congregations consistently engage in robust ministry, and some nearly always function with stunning timidity and confusion. But most congregations fall somewhere in-between these two stark examples. Some weeks your congregation will demonstrate focus and momentum, confidence and clarity. Other weeks it will exhibit disorientation and fatigue, apprehension and uncertainty. On some issues and opportunities, your congregation will respond with

11. Smith, *Howard Thurman: Essential Writings,* 150.

courage and precision. Yet other issues and opportunities that are no more complex or demanding will completely stump the band.

At its best, pastoral voice can read the temperature of a system,[12] identify likely dynamics at play, maintain an encouraging presence and perspective, and empower the congregation to perform its ministry. For example, if a congregation is in the doldrums of what appears to be a lifeless stretch, a minister with a strong pastoral voice can recognize that perhaps the congregation simply needs a break. As with humans, groups depend on a rhythm of work and rest. In this example, other dynamics may be at play as well, especially those related to loss and grief.[13] A minister who jumps to a conclusion about the congregation's indifference or lack of energy is probably oversimplifying things. The same can be said about how congregations embrace some opportunities and let others go. Such choices may reveal something that the congregation cannot articulate about its vocation, but becomes evident when members and leaders discuss various opportunities for ministry. Simply speaking, some opportunities will resonate and match more clearly the particular gifts and commitments of a congregation's members, some less so. A minister with a strong pastoral voice avoids quick and tidy judgments, not just because these assessments are often wrong, but also because they shut down conversations and close off possibilities. At its best, pastoral voice allows a minster to listen, learn, and then contribute. This following section highlights some of the ways that a student minister can do those things during his or her field education experience.

You will want to enter the congregation in the same manner that you move into the broader context that surrounds the congregation, with senses on full alert and a spirit open to what is present. While the access and participation on boards, councils, and leadership teams varies from one student ministry site to another, you will want to position yourself, as best as you can, to observe as many decision-making moments as possible. Careful observation will help you grasp what dynamics are at play, what values are guiding the conversation, and what moves discussions forward and what causes them to stall. In those moments, where do you sense God's presence and where do you believe others sense it? Is there evidence of the congregation trying to ground its work in the purposes

12. Heifetz et al, *Practice of Adaptive Leadership*, 159–61.

13. For a helpful discussion, see K. Brynolf Lyon and Dan P. Moseley's *How to Lead in Church Conflict: Healing Ungrieved Loss.*

of God? And where do you perceive subterfuge, distraction, and indifference? All of this information contributes to your ability to articulate what life is like in that congregation, at that present time.

Similar to the contextual study we discussed in chapter 2, learning about a congregation begins with a broad view, watches for common themes and patterns, and then leads to forming initial interpretations. Effective observation consists of four key steps—observing, listening, gathering, and interpreting[14]—but in order to arrive at a plausible picture of the congregation's life and ministry, you will need to step away from the dance from time to time and position yourself on the balcony.[15] This distancing is an exercise in self-differentiation. Uninterrupted involvement in the congregational dance will skew your perspective and your understanding of the dynamics at play.

Every congregation has a history, and frequently that history is written down and published. Occasionally, congregations will contract with a trained historian to capture that history, but often someone in the congregation without training attempts to do this. Many congregational histories provide important dates and snapshots of significant people and events, but fall short on two points. First, they rarely weave the dates, people, and events into a larger narrative that captures the significance of recurring themes, patterns, and connections. Second, intent on presenting the congregation in the best possible light, many histories do not deal with pivotal conflicts, even though those events can be particularly interesting and telling.

You will want to see if your congregation has a written history. At the very least, such a history will make you aware of the rough trajectory of the congregation. It will help you to gather some knowledge about the church's beginnings, under what circumstances that it formed, who the pastors have been and their average length of service, the buildings and property the church has occupied, and what the church has been known for through the years. (Remember, others telling the same congregational story may tell it differently from the way it is told by the writer of the history.) A written history may also help you to get an idea about people who were particularly influential in the life of the congregation, and why. This written history will help you identify helpful and interesting things about your church that you want to know more about.

14. See Appendix B for helpful ways to undertake these four steps.
15. Heifetz et al, *Practice of Adaptive Leadership*, 7–8.

In addition to a written history, every congregation also has a story, or perhaps several stories. Getting at those stories narrows the long, panoramic view of history, and can help you focus the picture such that it reveals what life is like in the congregation now. Indeed, some of these stories may be mentioned in the written history. While such stories may seem to be afterthoughts on the written page, in reality they may hold remarkable energy for members of your congregation. Like prisms, these stories can clarify the congregation's identity, values, and mission in sharp relief. You might think of these as signature stories, stories that reveal what lies at the heart of the congregation. For example, one such story, often told at Cedar Grove Baptist Church, functions to call the congregation together in conflicted times. It seems that Charley Hart strongly opposed the church giving up some of its building space to house a community agency, but the deacon board voted overwhelmingly in favor of doing so. Charley was disappointed, but saw it as the church's decision. He recognized that it was time to move on and to consider whatever proposal came next; he determined to consider the next project on its own merits rather than leverage past disappointments to exact revenge. When it came time to refurbish that office, Charley demonstrated his commitment to the church by leading the effort. It should be no surprise that Charley's story surfaces most every time Cedar Grove faces a tense situation or a difficult decision.

By contrast, sometimes an untold story influences the spirit and direction of the congregation. For example, the seminary interns at Soggy Valley Presbyterian Church always stumble over the same period of time when they attempt to write a congregational study paper for their field education class. Not a single student has been able to say much about the years 1985–1995 at Soggy Valley, despite interviewing several church members who were involved in the congregation during that time. The reason for this lapse is obvious when the historical records are pried open: the years 1985–1995 were a very troubling stretch for Soggy Valley because they were rife with financial malfeasance, sexual misconduct, destruction of personal property, and a severe breakdown in trust and communication among members of the congregation. The congregation essentially made an unwritten, unspoken pact never to discuss that decade. Some in the congregation may not be aware that they are skipping over those years during their interviews, while others do so with relentless intentionality. Sadly, the fallout continues from this shroud of silence:

severe nervousness appears in the congregation when any consequential conflict surfaces, which then allows the unspoken events of the past to paralyze the present.

In addition to histories and stories, certain categories can assess the trajectory, vibrancy, and dynamics of congregations. While these categories do not sum up a congregation any more fully than a Myers-Briggs Type Indicator completely captures an individual, they can nonetheless help you at least recognize patterns and tendencies. For example, a congregation begun five years ago will likely encounter a different set of issues than will a congregation that has just celebrated its centennial. A congregation with six hundred in worship will function differently than a congregation with sixty. A congregation on the town square may understand itself differently than a congregation located on a side street at the edge of town. These categories do not value one congregation over another, but simply help the observer to identify possible opportunities and issues at a given congregation.

Of all the ways to understand a congregational system and to discover your place in it, few things can substitute for positioning yourself well at the site and asking interesting, provocative questions. Such questions will truly help you discover how the system goes about its work or, in some cases, fails to go about its work. Again, provocative questions are not meant to provide you with an unambiguous diagnosis in the form of an easy-to-read printout, but, instead, such questions and the answers you receive are meant to help you discover certain patterns in the congregation and then prompt you to reflect on pastoral voice. You likely will develop some questions of your own, especially to follow-up on what you are observing, but the following ten questions are also a good start.

1. Where do you see conflict occurring in the congregation, what seems to be at the heart of the conflict, and how do those involved respond when conflict surfaces? Conflict can clarify and energize when facilitated well. It generates frustration, anger, resentment, and division when handled poorly.

2. What is the agility, both theologically and programmatically, of the congregation? Many mainline congregations exhibit theological nimbleness, but trying to mobilize them for life-giving ministry feels like trying to turn a cruise ship on a small pond. Larger, more conservative congregations are surprisingly agile with ministry and

programming initiatives, but often less nimble theologically.

3. What is the congregation's temperament toward experimentation and learning? A congregation that is not able to make provisional plans and learn from them, or one that is not willing to make some excellent mistakes,[16] usually will remain stuck and, further, will hunker down among themselves in perceived safety.

4. How does the congregation react to proposed change? A congregation that automatically accepts change or unthinkingly rejects it probably does not understand the issues involved; whereas a congregation that prayerfully weighs change for possibilities and the extent to which it fits with their particular vocation, spawns energy and clarity. Just remember, discernment is intended to be the means, not the end, of a process.

5. Where do you see triangulation in the congregation? Triangles occur everywhere, and in congregations the triangles include everything from the glory days of the past to the changing neighborhood of the present, and everybody from the bishop, the former pastor, a dissenter, and vulnerable ones in the congregation. Can you identify moments one person recruits another in order to side against a third person, event, or circumstance?

6. Where do conversations and processes stall in the congregation, what seems to be the common predictor of those breakdowns, and what, if anything, gets them going again? Can these moments be tied to other transitions and losses? Congregations differ as to what mobilizes and motivates them. Sometimes a group is simply awaiting more light to move forward, while others are perpetually stalled in darkness.

7. In the congregation, what evidence exists to prove they have adopted specific strategies and concrete plans? When a church engages in endless discussions that lead nowhere, frustrated people often cite a disconnect between intent and action as being the root of the problem. Indeed, most organizations are far better at diagnosing and interpreting a situation than they are at developing and implementing a plan that will address the situation.

8. How resilient and tough is the system in the congregation? Dan

---

16. Callahan, *Small, Strong Congregations*, 149.

Hotchkiss says that mainline churches bear the burden of a privileged past that has not toughened them for today's challenges.[17] Most churches are far more resilient than they claim or demonstrate, but it frequently takes a life-threatening challenge to the congregation to arouse that resiliency.

9. What triggers the system's anxiety in the congregation, and how does it play out? Anxiety can enter a congregation at various points, like a virus breaking into a body. Anxiety may surface in relation to a situation facing the congregation, but it also can be transported from an individual or family within the congregation. Once in, anxiety will land somewhere, often on the person, event, or circumstance that is perceived to be hobbling the congregation's efforts or threatening the congregation's status quo.

10. Which part of the brain dominates the life of your congregation, and is there an individual or leadership group that consistently functions as the neocortex for the congregation? Leaders emerge in congregations through formal and informal roles to calm the system and set the tone for its conversations.

As you develop an understanding of what life is like in your congregation, think about what is stirring in you. After all, as interesting as this analysis might be, you must connect these findings with what it raises for you and your pastoral identity. Just as with congregations, the discernment, diagnosis, and interpretation leads somewhere, or at least it is intended to lead somewhere. In your case, the dynamics you study during your field experience provides a frame in which you can think about your place in that system or a similar system. And, thus prepared, you can begin to visualize what will represent faithful and imaginative ministry for you.

HOW ENGAGING A SYSTEM GIVES RISE TO PASTORAL VOICE—SOME CASE STUDIES

Instead of devoting both case studies to examples of finding voice, which is the practice in the other chapters, this chapter includes one case study

---

17. Hotchkiss, *Governance and Ministry*, 27.

of abandoning voice. It is my hope that the contrast will illustrate the difference that leadership makes in an anxious system.

An Opportunity Missed at Larkspur Congregational Church

Through the first half of the twentieth century, Larkspur Congregational Church became a leading voice in its city, especially in the areas of Jewish-Christian relations, worship and the arts, ministries for the marginalized, and collaborative efforts between community organizations and church programming. Larkspur staked out theological and missional clarity in the 1920s, often over and against the Fundamentalism that was being embraced by many congregations and denominations. The thirty-five-year pastorate of Roy Pattell guided Larkspur toward a Progressive congregational stance, but he retired just as numerous civil rights initiatives were gaining traction across the United States.

In 1960, Larkspur called a new pastor who seemingly matched up well with the congregation's progressive commitments, but when racial riots broke out in Larkspur's city the congregation exhibited extreme uneasiness. Key voices in the congregation urged caution, and eventually the congregation withdrew altogether from the burgeoning civil rights conversation going on all around them. The highly coveted pastor who arrived in 1960 left less than three years later when it became evident to him that Larkspur was backing away from its identity. For three decades, the community had counted on Larkspur to be at the leading edge of justice issues, but the church became invisible during the racial strife that was engulfing its city and the nation. The city felt the loss of Larkspur's leadership and, over time, Larkspur lost as well. These few years in the early 1960s represented a turning point that shaped Larkspur's life for the subsequent forty years.

Larkspur's worship attendance dropped steadily over those four decades, before leveling off at about one-fourth of what it was at its peak. Over that same time, financial support declined as well. With fewer people and less money, the church made cuts in notable ministries and programs. In addition, Larkspur's most promising leaders—many of them professionals in the city—grew impatient with their congregational life, because members discussed issues but never acted upon them. Larkspur did not experience a split, but a drift. It was no longer clear to participants or newcomers if any energizing values and commitments remained at Larkspur.

In the midst of this decline and disarray, the congregation turned its efforts inward and worked to make its members happy. Members of the congregation would not have described the change in that way, but every action—or more accurately, inaction—pointed toward that goal. As a result, important conflicts that might have clarified Larkspur's identity were quickly set aside. From time to time, proposals and recommendations to focus and renew the congregation would surface, but the thought of even the slightest change brought out resistance in full force. With the well-differentiated leaders gone, and the threshold for pain so low, those who held firm to the do-nothing status quo had no one to challenge them. They held the congregation hostage, sometimes with nothing more than a deep sigh or a nodding head. The do-nothing faction consisted almost entirely of people whose lives away from the church demonstrated a similar level of malaise and imprecision.

During this time, Larkspur Congregational Church earned a reputation for calling pastors who were equally anxious and vague in their personal and professional lives. But in 2002, with yet another pastoral transition underway, a long overdue conversation broke open among leaders at Larkspur. Given the advancing average age of the members, some of the elder leaders recognized that the congregation could not sustain itself much longer, and so they pressed others to think whether they wanted to change or die. One elder compared the moment to the crossroads the church faced in 1960. "We withdrew from the community then and have never come out of hiding. We've only existed for ourselves ever since. We can stay on that path, but let's be clear where that takes us. The congregation will cease to exist sometime soon. Before we ever call another pastor, I think we need to be honest about what lies ahead for our church if we continue in this direction."

But instead of continuing the conversation, many members of the congregation scorned this elder leader. She had spoken the unspeakable, and in doing so had interrupted the happiness and denial at Larkspur. Unfortunately for the congregation's well-being and its future, the interruption was brief. After rationalizing that there was nothing wrong with being stuck, and then finding polite ways to label the elder as a troublemaker, the congregation returned to business as usual. In late 2002, the congregation called the Rev. Mary Margaret Sims to be their new pastor.

Early on in her tenure, Rev. Sims showed signs of differentiation, promise, and energy; but by the end of her second year she had become a custodian of the status quo and protector of the do-nothing faction. The system had overpowered her. It is worth noting that in her first year at Larkspur, two major justice issues surfaced in the city that, as the above-mentioned elder might have put it, "gave us the chance to reclaim our identity and voice in the community." But Rev. Sims and other leaders remained silent on both issues. Rev. Sims went on to reinforce the inward focus of the congregation by giving into her own obsessions with congregational minutia. In essence, she went out of her way to ensure everyone in the congregation was happy, an enterprise that took less and less time because the membership continued to dwindle.

A few years later, with an average worship attendance of twelve people in a sanctuary that seats six hundred, Larkspur formally concluded its ministry and sold its building to the Apostolic Word of God Fundamentalist Church, a congregation that already had two campuses in the city and was known for positions and commitments diametrically opposed to what characterized Larkspur's witness in its strongest days.

The elder who had spoken so strongly in 2002 grieved over what had happened. "For my own sanity and spiritual well being I left Larkspur several years ago, but I still feel the pain of this loss. Our city lost a light and voice that it desperately needs, but this was the path that the congregation chose. Several times I thought we would step up and reclaim what made Larkspur so vital in the early years, but we could not muster the nerve to do so."

Pastor Emma Stone and the Measure of Our Days

Emma Stone always felt rushed and behind. In her work as a pastor, she never had enough hours for what came her way. Early in her ministry she blocked out the occasional morning or afternoon to reflect, envision, and prioritize, but felt guilty for spending her time doing those things because she knew people were probably trying to contact her. She quit setting aside those times in her calendar, including preparation time for preaching, teaching, and leading worship, and began allowing whatever came up in a given week to dictate her use of time. When congregants expressed their appreciation for Emma responding so quickly to their calls, texts, and e-mails, she took that as a sign that her ministry was going well.

After some time, however, the leadership at her church confronted her with a different perspective. She was surprised to learn that, from their perspective, the congregation's overall life and witness were both deteriorating. They wanted Emma to reflect on how she was using her time. One member of the church council, a woman named Bonnie, put it this way: "Pastor, we recognize that you have had two or three funerals in one week on more than one occasion. Even one funeral in a week can nearly become that week's work. We know that. Many of us have been blessed by your presence and your words at these services.

"The question is not what else you can squeeze into a week when you have a funeral, much less two funerals, but rather how you spend your time in those weeks when you do not have a funeral or other important emergency? A lot of people have a hard time prioritizing their time. A lot of people only react to things that others have determined to be urgent and never get around to some really important tasks.[18] Or, some things may be important for someone else to do, either one of the part-time staff members or someone in the congregation, but they may not be important for you to do.

"We want to help you distribute your time according to the priorities of the pastoral office and the missional dreams of the congregation. We expect you to be present when there is a crisis, but we don't expect you to be in touch with all of us every day. Our congregation has experienced growth in several ways—spiritual, missional, numerical—but we cannot continue to enjoy that if you are not being intentional about your time. We are not interested in the status quo. We want to continue to grow and be a blessing to our town and to as much of the world as we can.

"The last thing we want to say is that we have committed two thousand extra dollars to your continuing education fund for workshops, books, or a ministry coach. We believe some exciting things are ahead for our partnership, and we want to make this investment in you as our pastor."

Emma was surprised that she had been confronted on this matter, and she was also a little embarrassed. But she recognized the concerns as real, and thought Bonnie had addressed them in a very sensitive and

18. Covey, *Seven Habits of Highly Effective People*, 150.

helpful way. The idea of a ministry coach appealed to her more than a workshop or conference. Over a period of two years, Emma worked with a coach who had a reputation for helping others become highly effective congregational leaders. The ministry coach helped her identify specific examples of urgent matters, and then differentiate urgent matters from important matters. Of course, some situations were both urgent and important, like crises with congregants or with the congregation as a whole, but Emma increasingly recognized that people in the congregation wanted her to get out of the way more often so that they could share in more of the ministry.

For example, Emma hated proofing the weekly newsletter, and she was not very good at it, but for three years she had committed most Tuesday mornings to that very activity. The part-time church secretary began giving Emma a list of the article titles for the newsletter each week for her review, but then the secretary and an editorial team comprised of involved church members and retired English teachers edited the articles, chased down details, and planned out what did and did not carry over from week to week.

Emma's ministry coach also helped Emma think about her pastoral oversight of the congregation. "In what ways," the coach asked her, "can you call forth the gifts and talents of others to support the ministry of the congregation?" The question became the filter through which she analyzed a lot of requests on her time. Doing so allowed her to realize a lot of opportunities that had been missed to that point. In particular, Emma focused more on fostering leadership among others. She did so through a series of small group discussions. In this capacity, she remained connected to the congregation, but also became a coach in her role as pastor because she led people to think about what energized them and how they might engage those possibilities in the congregation.

As both the council and her coach had recommended, Emma got away with a group of friends and colleagues three times a year for renewal and perspective. She used this time to think about what she was observing in the congregation, to share her perceptions with others who would give her honest feedback, and to think about how she could best use her time and energy in the coming months to lead the congregation toward continued growth. At one of those retreats, she realized that the congregation needed to call a part-time pastor for administration, communication, and visitation. Upon her return, she related this insight to the church leadership, and they quickly agreed to put her ideas into action.

In addition to helping the congregation flourish, Emma enjoyed more of her life and ministry. She was still busy—very busy, at times—and there were a few weeks when she felt rushed and behind, but even in those weeks she had attended to the most important aspects of pastoral leadership first. The result was clear. She was having a much greater impact than she had ever had before. A lot of the credit for her success belonged to the church council in general and to Bonnie in particular, whose devotion to the well-being of the congregation translated into attention, energy, and thoughtfulness that kept this particular system from sliding into a spiral of decline and diminishing ministry.

CULTIVATING VOICE—DEFINING SELF, CONNECTING WITH OTHERS

Helping groups experience and perform fulfilling ministry is an essential part of ministry. As a pastor, that is your place in a congregational system and now, as much as ever, your voice needs to be heard. Much of your work will occur with smaller groups, such as boards, teams, and task forces, but you also will be working with the congregation as one large group. Attempts to deny or dodge the importance of this work, or handling it sloppily, will undermine your ministry.

Situations arise occasionally when pastoral leadership can influence and even reform a system to some extent, but real change depends on more than isolated efforts or charismatic contributions. Increasing the focus and functioning of a system week-to-week and year-to-year comes from pastors and congregations sustaining a steady, consistent, prayerful, playful engagement with what matters most in their life together. To guide a congregation consistently, to delight in the presence of God, and to pursue God's purposes can take a toll on the pastor's emotional, spiritual, and physical health. In order to be effective leaders, pastors must regularly attend to their own well-being. Otherwise, systems swallow pastors and spit them out.

Edwin Friedman contended that basing pastoral performance on expertise is a game we cannot win.[19] Pastors hate to hear that. We are

19. Friedman, *Generation to Generation*, 2–6.

led to believe—sometimes by seminary professors!—that we could effect change in a congregation if we just had more knowledge or the latest pastoral technique. No matter how much expertise we amass, situations will present themselves for which we do not have enough knowledge or technique. Some pastors will encounter that limitation a few times and practically give up. Others will face the same circumstance and ask what can be learned or discovered about themselves, their congregation, and their context for ministry.

Congregations often believe that the answers to their troubles lie with expertise, and so they go in search of a new pastor with the best toolkit and the trendiest ideas. Friedman argued that the health of any system—family or congregation—depends on "the capacity of the family leader to define his or her own goals and values while trying to maintain a nonanxious presence within the system."[20] Both pastors and congregations hate to hear that their most pressing work is to gain clarity about themselves first. "If only the neighborhood had not changed," or "If only the culture wasn't so secularized," or "If only our last pastor had been a better preacher." Statements like these may hold just enough truth to divert their attention away from themselves and their own low level of functioning as a system. But the real truth is within: Moving forward with any impact or joy as a congregation begins with looking inward. The honest assessment that comes from that introspection may be hard to face, but experiencing increased health, enjoyment, and productivity depend on pastors and congregations functioning in more open, honest, self-aware, and intentional ways.

You will want to learn as much as you can about the many aspects of congregational leadership and administration, both while you are in seminary and throughout your ministry. But your pastoral voice first hinges on your ability to define yourself, your values, and priorities, and to execute them with exceptional clarity in every part of your life and ministry.

Consider the New Testament letter to Philemon. Paul and Philemon knew each other through the church in Colossae, so on one level this letter represents personal correspondence. But this letter is also addressed to the church that meets in Philemon's house, which indicates that Paul expects the particular matters he raises to be considered in the context

20. Ibid., 3.

of the life of the church. At some point, Paul encountered Philemon's runaway slave, Onesimus, and became quite fond of him. Despite Paul's fondness, he sent Onesimus back to Philemon. Paul writes this brief letter to Philemon to make a very specific request of him regarding Onesimus, and to affirm their ongoing relationship as brothers in Christ and partners in the gospel.

"Welcome him back as you would welcome me,"[21] Paul writes, and not as a runaway slave, but as "a beloved brother."[22] Paul clearly defines himself and his position by expressing his expectations. Paul essentially says, "I can only do what I can do, and I believe I have done what is appropriate for me to do. I am now asking you to do what is appropriate for you to do, though I certainly have no control over you or your actions." In doing so, Paul both exercises his own authority and honors Philemon.

And yet, as unambiguous as Paul's self-definition is, this exchange happens within a relationship that existed prior to Paul writing this letter, a relationship that Paul hopes will continue long after the letter is received. Paul expresses that connection to Philemon in many ways—through prayers of thanksgiving, with appreciation for Philemon's faith and ministry, and by grounding this appeal in the spirit and practice of *agape* love. Paul further affirms the ongoing relationship with Philemon and the church by saying that he hopes to visit them soon.

We do not know what eventually happened between Paul, Philemon, and Onesimus, but the story demonstrates the self-differentiation needed in order for a discerning, engaging pastoral voice to flourish in a congregational system. Paul exercises self-definition, but remains connected to Philemon and the church at Colossae. Paul's hope is clear, but Paul also acknowledges an appropriate boundary between the two men and chooses not to overstep his place and encroach upon decisions that rightly belong to Philemon.

What will help you cultivate a pastoral voice that reflects this kind of self-differentiation? First, arrive at and sustain exceptional personal, pastoral, and theological clarity. In thinking about personal clarity, review the questions about your congregational system (consult the second section of this chapter), and then from those scenarios identify your growing edges. For example, how can you more consistently form relationships of

21. Phil 1:17.
22. Phil 1:16.

integrity and transparency in the church of your ministry? What will help you become a nonreactive facilitator in moments of intense conflict? What will prepare you to function as the neocortex of a congregational system?

This book focuses on how pastoral voice grows out of clarity with context, theology, pastoral roles, personal well-being, and systemic dynamics. Pastoral clarity with those things will foster clarity among your congregation about its identity, values, and mission. However, that clarity, both on the part of the pastor and the congregation, must lead to value-laden and commitment-guided practice in order for it to have any real and lasting impact. Achieving these goals requires that you and your congregation intentionally distribute your time. Time management is not just about making sure we get everything done. Rather, it means prioritizing our time according to our ministry commitments instead of merely reacting to whatever demand that presents itself. Some matters do not warrant an investment of time and energy. "Urgent" matters like unimportant phone calls and e-mails cut into time that should be set aside for important matters, like study, prayer, and visioning. Note the distinction between *urgent* and *important*. We, ministers of the church, are not engaging just any group of volunteers in a yet-to-be-agreed-upon agenda. We are the church, seeking to bear witness to the presence and purposes of God. In the midst of a string of committee meetings, wandering conversations, and endless details, it is easy to lose sight of that.

Most pastors know to respond to a crisis in the congregation, but they do not carve out time to arrive at a long view of a given situation. As a result, congregations experience identity and mission drift from which many do not recover. By contrast, let us consider an exceptional minister, named Rev. Blakemore. Several weekday mornings he blocks out up to three hours for study, sermon preparation, and worship planning. Once every month he commits an afternoon to getting feedback from a small group of friends about where he believes God is calling the congregation to go in the next five to ten years, and how the congregation might get there. He is not available to others during those times, and he turns off his phone and computer. To ensure these times are protected, he clearly apportions the hours of the day: He works from his home in the morning, makes hospital and home calls in the early afternoon, keeps office hours the rest of the afternoon, and attends meetings two nights a week. As a result, Rev. Blakemore is known as an exceptional preacher and teacher. He is also perceived as a leader because he frequently weaves congregational priorities and ministry initiatives into meetings. Doing so shifts the tone and substance of the meetings from a dreaded waste of time to a discussion about the well-being and the future of the congregation.

Second, find what renews you, believe that you are as worthy of renewal as anybody else, and schedule time to do what renews you in the same way you schedule any and every other commitment. When you enter it in your electronic calendar, designate it with a different color—maybe your favorite color—and when the program asks if this is a recurring event, click "Yes, every week!" Set the reminder for your time of renewal with a song that you associate with happy and fun times. And then do whatever it is that renews you. Nobody in your congregation will believe you have a Sabbath until you believe you do. When you believe it and practice it, the congregation will believe it, too.

Ministry involves a high level of emotional, physical, and spiritual health. There is a relentlessness to ministry that many seminarians do not anticipate. Not only does every week include a working Sunday, which is something that people know and yet are strangely unprepared for, but every week brings an onslaught of opportunities and challenges. Individuals will have need for their pastor every day of the week, and the congregation as a whole will always be trying to turn the next corner, no matter how many you have successfully navigated already. The stamina, discipline, and focus required to live from the center of your values and priorities will be tested at every turn. Constant delays and diversions will threaten to obstruct your agility and will endeavor to sidetrack your efforts. It will not be personal. It is simply what systems do.

Taking time away from the congregational system to replenish yourself is an act of love for the congregation and an expression of devotion for what the congregation wants to accomplish. Unless you keep a regular commitment to be good to yourself, you cannot be present, playful, and excited in the midst of the rigors of ministry. It does not do anybody any good if the pastor is more burned out than the congregation. On the other hand, it does all of us a world of good if the pastor continues to take delight in his or her work and in the congregation he or she serves.

To repeat, you must take direct, consistent, and intentional responsibility for your self-care. Without this self-care, you will do more than deplete your reserves or fall into depression. You will lose your pastoral voice. Without making time to replenish, you will develop something like spiritual laryngitis, a weakening of the voice, something that can become so painful that you can barely speak or, if you do speak, all your words will sound the same and nobody, including you, will pay much attention to what you have to say.

Third, stay current in your relationships. This will come easier for you if you are making time for your physical, emotional, and spiritual well-being. In the previous chapter of this book, we noted that staying current in your personal life is a key element for maintaining your pastoral voice. Staying current with your relationships in the congregation is equally important. This does not mean chasing around after everybody and making sure that all of them are your BFF (best friend forever). Rather, it refers to tending to your relationships like you would a well-groomed garden— with an appreciation for what is beautiful in a relationship, while paying timely attention to any threatening issues or unfinished business. Jesus said, "So when you are offering your gift at the altar, if you remember that your brother or sister has something against you, leave your gift there before the altar and go; first be reconciled to your brother or sister, and then come and offer your gift." [23]

You will accumulate, as well as inflict, a lot of nicks and bruises during the course of your pastoral ministry. Sometimes you may experience incredible betrayal or intense persecution, but more often a congregation's resistance to your leadership will feel more like you are being stoned with marshmallows. If you are emotionally exhausted or spiritually depleted, such an assault may feel like persecution. But, in truth, the ire of a congregation rarely rises to that standard. If you respond to resistance as persecution, though, you can expect more of it. If you respond to pushback with exceptional personal and pastoral clarity, your reaction likely will open new conversations and possibilities for your life and ministry together.

Forgiveness is essential to vital ministry. Otherwise, the togetherness becomes unbearably dishonest or superficial, and both parties will lose interest in staying connected. The inability to forgive is a contributing factor in unnecessarily short pastorates. You will not be able to lead a congregation to attend to its present business if you are still living in the slight of last week's board meeting, or last month's duplicity by a deacon, or last year's disappointment about a ministry proposal. Nor will you be able to demonstrate the kind of agility and nimbleness needed for

23. Matt 5:23–24.

effective pastoral leadership if you are dragging heavy burdens of resentment, frustration, and loss behind you. On the other hand, pastors who immerse themselves in life-giving patterns and commit to healthy, long-term relationships often can facilitate lively conversations and translate a congregation's quirks and passions into gospel ministry.

7

Finding and Embodying Voice

The young man or woman writing today has forgotten the problems of the human heart in conflict with itself which alone can make good writing.[1]

—WILLIAM FAULKNER

FROM VOICE TO AGENDA

IF YOU READ THE previous chapters, then you know that your pastoral voice is a product of the particulars of your life and ministry. Each important event of your life is filled with promising possibilities and genuine concerns to shape or strengthen your pastoral voice. Your work, however, is not only to understand each event and to then utilize it to this end, but to understand how each event informs and influences the others. At times, your life events will interact in complementary ways, but just as often they will do so in complicating, even contradictory, ways.

Perhaps the best way to describe this phenomenon is to illustrate it. Hence, I will soon introduce you to Kathleen, who serves as pastor of North Hinton Community Church (NHCC). She began service in this church after graduating three years ago from seminary. From the beginning of her tenure at NHCC, Kathleen has attempted to translate her pastoral voice into a clear, hopeful pastoral agenda for the sake of her congregation's identity, mission, and vitality.

1. Faulkner, "Banquet Speech."

But before I tell you more about Kathleen and her ministry, I first need to provide you with some general observations about pastoral leadership. In some contexts, the word "agenda" is synonymous with an autocratic, unrestrained, unaccountable power grab. Many of us have witnessed pastoral leadership that seeks to manipulate a congregation at every turn. But, more often, pastoral leaders do not step up to fulfill, in particular, the teaching and oversight roles of their pastoral office. Rather than calling a congregation to engage its mission and contribute to conversations that result in clear, hopeful, and concrete plans to translate into action, more than a few pastors take the easier, safer path of deferring to the system's impulses to avoid risk, pain, and adventure. It appears that, in those cases, keeping everyone happy and comfortable comprises the pastoral agenda. Such an agenda has little concern or investment for empowering the congregation to fulfill its vocation. In some cases, frustrated, drifting congregations practically beg for guidance and support, and still do not receive it from their pastors.

Further, a minister can have a pastoral agenda and yet embrace a collaborative ministry that values the gifts of everyone. These are not contradictory ideas. When a pastor abdicates his or her roles and responsibilities, that ministry is no longer collaborative. Indeed, such a ministry only includes the ever-important gifts of the laity, but not the gifts and wisdom of the pastor. A pastoral agenda, however, should not dominate congregational conversations; rather it should actively facilitate them. One of the key pastoral roles is that of clarifying, challenging, and contributing to congregational conversations about the commitments and practices that are at the heart of a Christian community. In other words, a pastoral agenda guides a congregation toward having the same mind as was in Christ Jesus,[2] so that it will intentionally participate in God's desire for the world.

The following snapshots are meant to illustrate these roles and agendas by way of one particular pastor, Kathleen, who negotiates the always present components that we have discussed already in this book—context, faith story, pastoral roles, personal journey, and systemic dynamics—and how those components complement and conflict with one another. Kathleen does not step occasionally into the conversation about context, or from time to time delve into the beliefs and practices of her

2. Phil 2:5.

church tradition, or intermittently live with who she is as a person. These are not separate, unrelated perspectives that Kathleen seeks to bring back together, that is, to integrate; they are experiences that occur concurrently and interpret each other in every moment.

Important conflicts surface when the dynamics of these interlocking components send contradictory signals to the congregation. For example, the faith story may call the congregation to adopt a risk-laden ministry plan in order to bless the community, but a timid congregational system will fight those plans at every turn. The congregation might even formally adopt the ministry plan, but not be able to implement it because of the anxiety that plagues the congregation. Pastoral leadership occurs in the midst of dynamics that, at the very least, must be negotiated and, often, work against each other.

As individuals, most of us ignore or avoid our internal conflicts, and many congregations follow suit. But congregations cannot adopt priorities and develop strategies for life-giving ministry without navigating the sometimes harsh waters that these conflicts create. William Faulkner contends that, for a writer, it is helpful for the human heart to be in conflict with itself. And what is true for such a writer is also true for us as individuals. Out of those conflicts of the human heart we determine what really matters, and through that determination decide to what we should give our time and energy. It follows that ministers and congregations, in turn, benefit from spending time at these various points of conflict. Doing so allows a congregational vocation to become coherent, and enables ministry initiatives to clarify. Simply put, congregations and ministers who do not work through conflict create irrelevant plans that neither speak to any particular situation nor take into account related issues and opportunities. Engaging in conflict is time-consuming and difficult work that will stretch the most imaginative and patient pastor. Ministers who do not take into account the conflicts of the big picture will find that, in most cases, their ministry plans, as intriguing as they may be, will have little impact on the congregation or community.

In order to translate these general observations into the specific examples, let us return our attention to Kathleen and her church, North Hinton Community Church (NHCC). NHCC is an Anglo congregation with marginal ties to the United Church of Christ. At one time, NHCC was a program-size congregation with three hundred and fifty in worship. Today, NHCC's average worship attendance hovers around ninety. NHCC is located on the north side of Hinton, a Midwestern city with a population of 85,000. Keep these facts in mind as you consider the ways in which Kathleen navigates the conflicting dynamics at NHCC. It is difficult and dangerous to make judgments about the pastoral work of a colleague, and this is especially true when information is limited, as it is here. A fair consideration of Kathleen's motivations and actions requires that the observer have a much more complete picture than what I can provide in the single chapter of a book. Nonetheless, it is my hope that this glimpse into the particulars of one person's life and ministry can provide you with an opportunity to see yourself in pastoral ministry and help you think about how you will respond to the many opportunities and challenges you will someday encounter.

As you will see, even when a conflict can be framed by two dynamics, others remain present and contribute to the uncertainty about how best to handle the issues at hand.

SIGNS OF KATHLEEN'S EMERGING PASTORAL VOICE

Understanding Where You Are. The NHCC search committee that interviewed Kathleen gave her an extensive tour of the three-story church building, which had been built sixty years ago. But this tour said little about the neighborhood. The interview itself took place at a private residence, located nearly ten miles from the church building. Kathleen asked the search committee, which was made up of six people sixty years of age or older and one young woman in her twenties, about where the members and regular participants of the congregation lived in relation to the church.

"Fifty percent of our members live in the church's zip code," a woman quickly replied, sounding as if she was reading directly from a demographic study. "Forty more percent live in contiguous zip codes." The tidy and somewhat impatient response caused Kathleen to suspect that other candidates had asked this question, and that the search committee was growing tired of answering it.

"I noticed some buildings nearby the church appeared to be abandoned," Kathleen started. "It looks like an area that has seen its share of change and loss. Is that a fair statement?"

"Four of us grew up within three blocks of the church," said Sam, a distinguished looking man in a suit and tie. "Now we hold most of our evening meetings away from the church because of the crime in the area. Our old high school is one of the abandoned buildings. The middle school was converted ten years ago to a warehouse for the school system. Every year there's a fight to keep the elementary school open. Several of us carry a good bit of sadness about the whole situation."

"Has there been a shift in the population as well?" Kathleen already knew the answer to this question, but wanted to hear how the search committee would respond.

"There has," Sam replied. "Most may live in nearby zip codes, but a couple of miles in any direction makes a big difference. This has been a racially integrated neighborhood for decades, so it's nothing new to have whites, blacks, and Hispanics living alongside one another. Several international professors from the university used to live in this area, too. The north side of Hinton once was a culturally rich area, especially for a city this size. The change is socioeconomic. With a poorer, less educated group of people have come urban problems that we are not accustomed to seeing." Everyone nodded in agreement to Sam's concise description of the context.

Even before NHCC extended an official call to Kathleen, she was already thinking about ways for NHCC to bless its community and to be blessed by it. "What," she wondered to herself after the interview, "could NHCC learn from the people who now live within a few blocks of the church?"

After Kathleen became the pastor of NHCC, she pondered this question more deeply. In an effort to discover an answer, she observed people in the community and listened to them. She often did this by visiting a favorite lunch diner called Brooking's. To Kathleen it seemed that Brooking's was the one place in the neighborhood where there was a real connection between the past and present. Former and current residents of the neighborhood ate side by side in a friendly and sometimes energized environment, especially when discussing the local, much loved college basketball team. Kathleen wanted to know more about how Brooking's became the place that attracted a diversity of area residents and hosted community conversations.

Connecting with the Greater Faith Story. Kathleen knew that NHCC was a holdover from the old days of modern Christendom. She understood that NHCC came from an era that assumed churches and their communities shared mutually beneficial interests and concerns. The two institutions formed a social safety net and regularly called on each other for support, and this close connection meant that congregations rarely critiqued or challenged their community's laws and norms, even those that were obviously discriminatory and injurious. In this regard, NHCC was a good citizen. It even served as a community center at times. But the identity of the congregation at NHCC was not deeply shaped by biblical themes and theological underpinnings. As a result, when the schools, the small family businesses, and the professionals left the area, NHCC had difficulty understanding its own identity.

With these facts in mind, Kathleen began to study the original social contract that NHCC had struck with its community. When the church had first opened its doors, the neighbors of the church and the members of the congregation shared very similar backgrounds, views, and commitments. Now, however, the two had little in common. While it was true that NHCC financially supported its denominational outreach causes and a number of local efforts in Hinton, Kathleen recognized that the congregation at NHCC seemed completely lost when it came to getting to know its neighbors or thinking creatively about how to express its ministry in the neighborhood.

Kathleen began her work of reconnecting NHCC to the community by first helping NHCC understand itself in light of the Christian story. "What does it mean for us to be church in this time and place?" she frequently asked herself. A few months after arriving at NHCC, Kathleen began a series of small group conversations that explored this question, but she did so with an interesting caveat. Instead of leading her parishioners in a discussion of what she believed it meant to be the church in this time and place, she encouraged the group participants to name the ways that the congregation currently lived out its vocation as the church and practiced the Christian faith.

Interestingly, a particular story from Jeremiah 32 began to frame the situation. In that story, Jerusalem was again under siege. In the midst of a hopeless military and political situation at the hands of the Babylonians, Jeremiah did an almost unbelievable thing. He bought some land. Recall that this was a time when those people being carried to exile by the Babylonians thought they would never again return to Jerusalem. In the realm of real estate, Jeremiah's actions might be compared to a refugee who purchases a townhouse in a war zone, or a peasant who buys back a family farm during an exodus caused by a famine. Jeremiah's purchase was, in truth, a theological announcement. Not all was lost, he proclaimed. There would be life in our land again.

This story from Jeremiah became a key biblical reference for NHCC as the congregation decided not only to reaffirm its commitment to remain in the neighborhood, but to invest in it as well. It was not clear at first what that commitment might look like, but prayerful conversations led the congregation to ask, "What do you suppose God desires for this area of town and how might we participate in that?" A new identity was slowly being born, one shaped by a faith story with life, hope, and mutuality at its center.

Embracing the Vocation of Pastor. Kathleen listened and observed a lot during her first six months at NHCC. She visited with people in their homes. She ate lunch with others. She got to know the people of her congregation individually and tried to understand how they viewed their congregation. These people opened up to Kathleen, and often told her stories about when they were most proud of their church and when their participation at NHCC was the most fulfilling.

In addition to listening to the stories of church members, Kathleen became a roving listener in the neighborhood. She stopped in at Brooking's at different times of the day, visited with the elementary school principal, became acquainted with the director of a jobs bank down the street from the church, and stopped by the homeless shelter from time to time. She walked to these places anytime she could and quickly became a recognizable person in the neighborhood. In doing so, Kathleen heard some strange and discouraging comments. The school principal thought the church had closed a few years ago. Some people she talked with in a nearby park thought the church was a library. Others simply made comments that suggested the church just kept to itself.

Kathleen devoted a significant amount of time to worship and sermon preparation. The expectation of excellence associated with being a program-size congregation had carried over from the past to the present. Fortunately, an endowment for worship and music, which had been established years ago, still provided a few hundred dollars each month to underwrite guest musicians and special events. Kathleen wanted the congregation to enjoy its praise of God so much that they would not want to miss the worship service; but she also viewed worship as a time when her preaching could explore the intersections between the neighborhood, the congregation, and the Christian faith.

A sermon that Kathleen gave from Jeremiah 18 resonated deeply with some members of the congregation. Some even considered that particular sermon to be the most honest words ever spoken from the NHCC pulpit. Conveying what Jeremiah had witnessed at the potter's house, Kathleen described a potter reworking a vessel that had spoiled in his hands. With great pastoral sensitivity, Kathleen acknowledged the grief that many in the congregation had felt for years. "Things have changed around here," she said. "Perhaps we think the neighborhood is the spoiled vessel. Perhaps it is our church that is the spoiled vessel. But remember, that is only part of the story. "He reworked it into another vessel, as seemed good to him."[3] The new vessel wasn't like the old one. Our life in this area of Hinton isn't going to be like it was twenty or thirty years ago, but is there some reworking that is possible here? Maybe even some reworking in the church that is already underway? I can imagine the hands of God at work reshaping the clay. I think I can also hear in that Jeremiah story a call for us to put our hands on the clay and to participate in the reshaping of this community."

This message struck such a deep chord because Kathleen had listened to each person with genuine care and concern. And, through her concerted efforts, she had earned the trust of the congregation. Afterward, several people sought out Kathleen because they were eager to see where these conversations about God, church, and community might lead.

Discovering Who You Are as a Person in Ministry. The things that frustrated Kathleen the most at NHCC matched several of her own personal challenges. For instance, Kathleen was often unable or unwilling to say "No." As often as not, this meant she could not give any one project the time, attention, and specificity it needed to flower into a promising ministry. In seminary, she had received assignments with clear parameters and due dates. Part of her transition to congregational ministry is learning how to allocate her time on most days. With no deadlines or end of the semester looming, everything seemed very open-ended to her at first. While she has made improvements, to this day she grapples, often unsuccessfully, with setting priorities and following through. As a result, some of her excellent work in understanding and connecting with the

---

3. Jer 18:4.

neighborhood did not lead to concrete ideas for ministry as soon as they might otherwise have.

Likewise, NHCC still keeps ideas for ministries on the table for discussion, even if they do not have resources or even interest to follow through. Instead of committing to three or four ministries and doing them well, the congregation discusses dozens of possibilities at length without ever acting on any of them. Left unchecked, Kathleen realizes that her shortcomings in this area will contribute to the struggles of NHCC to define itself as a congregation. It is also true that an already grief-stricken congregation is not quick to voluntarily give up things that have been popular or effective in the past. Together, Kathleen and the congregation struggle through their shortcomings.

Toward the end of the first year at NHCC, Kathleen recognized that she was overextended emotionally and that she had not devoted sufficient time to prayer, study, and play. The lack of emotional and spiritual renewal took its toll physically on her. She was fatigued, she had poor eating habits, and she needed physical exercise. Her condition was such that she even considered leaving NHCC, perhaps to seek an associate ministry position at a larger congregation.

Kathleen, who is a single woman living six hundred miles from most of her family, had not worked to develop a rich social life outside of the church. Most of her acquaintances were ministry colleagues. While she appreciated them, they did little to ease the sense of isolation that ministry can bring. Kathleen knew she had to develop interests and friends beyond the church in order to regain a healthy balance to her life. And so she sought out opportunities in Hinton that appealed to her—dance, yoga, pottery, and improvisational comedy. In addition, she set aside time to visit museums in a larger city, which was about forty-five minutes away.

And so Kathleen stayed on as the pastor of NHCC. Three years elapsed. She had control of her personal life, and she felt that her ministry was strong. However, because of this focused hard work, Kathleen discovered a humbling truth about herself: She does not deal well with criticism. And because she wants to avoid criticism, she says "yes" when she really wants to say "no"; and then struggles to set the boundaries between her personal and professional life. At some level, she knows that she overextends herself with the hope that people in the church will cut her some slack. And they usually do. But Kathleen had been purchasing those free passes at a huge expense to her personal well-being. NHCC had been in decline for forty years, meaning that it will take years, several painful moments, and a lot of creativity and focus in order for that forlorn congregation to become vibrant again. Even if it happens—and there is no guarantee that it will—Kathleen has come to realize that she must nevertheless develop a keener sense of her capacities and limitations.

Finding Your Place in the System. Geoff retired as the long-time NHCC pastor five years ago. He stayed away from the congregation during his predecessor's tenure, and returned during the interim period that preceded Kathleen's arrival. During Kathleen's interviewing process, the search committee did not mention any concerns they had about Geoff. But since then, some of them have told Kathleen about Geoff and that his relationship with the congregation is "complicated."

Fifteen years ago, when significant shifts were taking place in the neighborhood and NHCC was attracting only a nominal number of new members, Geoff tried to persuade the congregation to enter into a strategic planning process. But key leaders resisted Geoff's ideas, saying that a visioning process was not necessary. After all, worship attendance was above three hundred per Sunday, the building needed no immediate maintenance, and finances were strong.

Even so, Geoff said then that they needed to think strategically about the future from a position of strength and health, not after irreversible decline was underway. Geoff was told to drop the idea, but he did not stop pushing it until he was on the verge of being fired. Only then did he relent. Geoff stayed ten more years as pastor at NHCC, and he never mentioned it again. The congregation had bought his silence. Geoff allowed them to stay in their comfort zone, but most of what Geoff had predicted came true. Worship attendance declined by half, mostly through death and inactivity of aging members, and the congregation stopped paying attention and participating in its immediate context. The congregation found itself smaller, poorer, older, isolated, and adrift.

Now, these many years later, Geoff is back in the fold. When Kathleen arrived at NHCC, Geoff privately pressed her to address all of the concerns that he did not address. All the while, he enjoyed the very public status of a returning beloved pastor. And why not? He demanded nothing of the congregation, and the congregation demanded nothing of him. Kathleen was unprepared for this triangle and, because she was new to the church, she was not able to identify people in the congregation with whom she could ally. In addition, Kathleen did not quickly pick up on how this triangle fueled the resistance in the congregation to the ministry initiatives that she and others wanted to explore and implement.

"Just focus on things here in the congregation," members told Kathleen.

"But what happens in the neighborhood impacts the church, doesn't it?" she countered.

"In some small way, maybe, but we can't control what happens around us," they told her.

"I'm not saying we can control anything," Kathleen replied, "but doesn't being a vibrant community of faith involve being sent into the world to bear witness to God's love and healing? Isn't there something at the heart of the gospel that calls us to care about more than just ourselves?"

"Kathleen, honey," said the condescending board chair, "you work for us, the people in this church. That's where your focus needs to be."

The NHCC system was so powerful that it often caused its leaders to work against the church's best interest. Anxiety about changes in the neighborhood forced the congregation to focus inwardly, to be quickly suspicious about anything new or different, and to suppress potential conflict at every turn. The meddling of the retired pastor both confirmed and amplified this mindset. Kathleen, who was already tired from attempting too much, found the dysfunctional relationships and self-defeating congregational strategies both discouraging and exhausting.

NAVIGATING THE CONFLICTS INHERENT IN PASTORAL VOICE

Kathleen rather quickly found herself in choppy waters as she tried to hold these dynamics in creative tension with one another. She believed that opportunities existed for NHCC to reclaim their faith commitments and find new ways to embody and express them, but sorting out these dynamics was like diving under a desk into a tangle of hundreds of computer cables and then trying to find where they connected and how they worked together. The situation taxed Kathleen's capacity for assessment and action. She believed that facilitating three particular conflicts (described below) could create opportunities for the congregation to experience renewed focus and energy. As difficult as this was at times, Kathleen sought to remain present and engaged with these three conflicts with the hope of finding voice in the midst of them.

Conflict Number One: Pastoral Roles and Community Context. Kathleen quickly realized that her seminary training prepared her well for a number of pastoral roles within the church—leading worship, preaching and teaching, developing curriculum—but offered little about how to help the congregation understand and engage its setting for ministry. She was especially stymied when thinking about what it meant to bridge congregation and community in her role as a pastor. Her pathway and duties might be clearer if she were a community organizer or a social worker, but she was a pastor. She wondered, then, what work fell to her. She endeavored to find out.

Even though Kathleen believes that the gospel calls the church to a healing, reconciling, life-giving ministry in the world, and even though she understands her calling to be a minister in the community as well as the church, she was tempted to withdraw from the community, just as the congregation had done, perform the ministry she knew how to perform, and hope someone else would come forward to address the challenges of the area around the church. She simply did not know where to start, yet she knew that as long as this conflict was left unexplored the congregation would continue to turn inwardly upon itself until it would finally conclude its ministry. Because Kathleen and others believed that the NHCC story was one worth sustaining, she devoted herself to developing pastoral clarity and agility at this crucial intersection.

Kathleen found voice in this area in three ways. First, she allowed the guiding faith commitments of her own life to shape and focus her ministry as a pastor. Few commitments held more resonance to her than the prophets' calls to justice and fairness. Second, she visited congregations in similar settings to learn about the concrete and specific ways that they were practicing resurrection in their communities. Kathleen discovered that all of those congregations had developed highly focused ministries through hopeful experimentation and more than a few failures. Third, she got out of her office and built relationships with other community stakeholders. As a result, NHCC became a place where important conversations occurred. Kathleen had envisioned that the church could be a place, not unlike Brooking's, where people with diverse backgrounds and perspectives could come together and commit to common work. The congregation did not always participate in those projects once they were underway, but the congregational leaders increasingly understood that facilitating some of those conversations was a part of NHCC's vocation.

Conflict Number Two: Faith Story and Congregational System. Kathleen recognized that the members of NHCC understood that justice and service are at the core of the Christian faith, but she also recognized that this same congregation rarely moved beyond the limits of its system to enact its faith. Quite good at diagnosing situations, Kathleen saw that NHCC was not able to implement ministry initiatives that expressed its core commitments. Doing so required a systemic nimbleness that it could not, or perhaps would not, muster. Kathleen found herself working with a church council that could affirm that practicing resurrection was at the heart of the Christian witness, but failed to see how little resurrection it actually practiced.

Kathleen found that people at NHCC talked about the church's outreach to the community, but in doing so they often unknowingly exaggerated their efforts and the impacts these efforts made. On the one hand, she found that they talked regularly about providing safety, food, and vaccinations to the vulnerable children of the world, but they could not decide whether and how to deploy volunteers to an elementary school two blocks away that was in constant and critical need of contributions of various kinds. The upshot was that when an opportunity presented itself to support a conference mission trip to Congo, the church council decided not to make a contribution or send anyone because, they maintained, charity starts at home. Examples like this showed Kathleen that this congregation was so focused on its own survival that it rarely was able to look beyond itself. Fear and grief had all but paralyzed its already low functioning governance structure. It never occurred to most people in the congregation that looking beyond itself might be a way to survive and even thrive as a church. But this notion occurred to Kathleen.

In an effort to save itself, the church council finally heeded the advice of their retired pastor, Geoff, and decided to launch a strategic planning process. They contracted with a conference minister to guide them. At the second meeting, the leadership team decided to devote several months to rewriting the constitution and bylaws of NHCC. This made perfect sense to a generation of people whose institutional loyalty caused them to seek organizational answers to every situation, regardless of whether the questions or issues were rooted in organizational problems. By contrast, Kathleen first wanted the congregation to discern its calling and identify key ministry initiatives, and then implement an organizational structure that would empower that ministry. But she could not convince anyone else of the value of that approach. When possible, Kathleen encouraged the visioning team to think in terms of a minimal, provisional organizational structure that the congregation could operate with for two years. In this way, the organization could better match ministry and resources. However, the manager types that dominated this committee could only think in terms of constitutional revision. The conference minister sided with Kathleen. He reminded members of this committee that by focusing on the constitution and bylaws first they were hemming themselves in and would miss opportunities and possibilities for ministry. The conference minister received an e-mail a few days later notifying him that his services were no longer needed.

Down but not out, instead of trying to move a pastoral agenda through a visioning process, Kathleen took it upon herself to identify opportunities for ministry in the neighborhood around the church. She found that the elementary school needed tutors, that people who went to the jobs bank needed help with their resumes, and that the homeless shelter needed a clothing closet. From participating in small group conversations, Kathleen knew of several people in the congregation who had a particular interest in helping out in each of those areas. Within two months, Kathleen and key leaders had implemented incremental, specific ministries with these neighborhood agencies and, in the process, had involved nearly thirty people from the congregation. The energy from these ministry initiatives spilled over into the church council and began to reshape its deliberations. Indeed, NHCC received an infusion of energy that enlivened its worship, learning, fellowship, and service.

Conflict Number Three: Personal Journey and Systemic Dynamics. Kathleen found that an effective pastor must have an enormous amount of stamina. She was reminded of this truth during conversations when the congregational values were subverted by endless discussions about matters that could and should have been handled easily and quickly. For example, over the course of four consecutive months, the only items discussed at the church council meetings had to do with the purchasing of a new copier, buying new fixtures for the third floor women's restroom, and removing a tree at the back of the church property. At the conclusion of these four months, a decision had not been made on any of these matters. These discussions dominated the room and pushed larger questions about the role of NHCC in context of its present community completely off the table.

The genuinely lovely people who were keepers of the status quo made it difficult for Kathleen to remain enthused and engaged. Kathleen's discomfort with criticism had led to extreme risk aversion in the past, which then caused considerable frustration among those congregational leaders who wanted NHCC to find its ministry again. Kathleen dealt almost daily with the temptation to let discomfort with conflict to squash her guiding faith commitments and some very good pastoral instincts. It was also evident that Kathleen, perhaps because of her youthful age or lack of life experience, regularly underestimated the impact of grief on congregational processes.

Kathleen overcame the temptation to remain quiet and passive by revisiting why she pursued ordained ministry in the first place. The possibility of shaping purposeful community life had long ago captured her imagination. The intrigue of working with people of diverse gifts and experiences continued to excite her. She also arrived at a point when she was able to understand that disagreement is not the same as persecution—a new thought for her!

During her second year, Kathleen caught her breath and began choosing more carefully what received her time and energy. She also realized that NHCC was much too large a ship to turn in one fell swoop, and so she began identifying smaller pieces of ministry in which she and other interested leaders could have an immediate impact with little or no financial commitment from the church council. In fact, while Kathleen tended to some necessary organizational work, much of her energy was spent on projects that did not involve or need the approval of the church council. Before long, the church council was essentially saying to the congregation, "Wait for us, we are your leaders!"

Kathleen's deepening sense of call to NHCC led her to venture into new territory as a person and pastor. She found herself encouraging the congregation to relax, dream, and experiment, even though she felt quite vulnerable when they actually did those things. For all of her disdain for congregational administration, she became nervous when the visioning team took her advice (two years after it was offered) and suspended the constitution and bylaws indefinitely. That move helped both Kathleen and the congregational leaders think afresh about what administration was necessary for them to support lively worship, deep learning, rich

fellowship, and joyful service. It also served to streamline some processes, focus the congregation more outwardly, and free people to engage in
ministries that before would have been vetoed almost immediately.

KATHLEEN'S JOURNEY TO VOICE CONTINUES

From the beginning, NHCC and the Hinton community called forth
something in Kathleen that would not die. Kathleen's energy and hopefulness had animated a historic, highly traditional congregation and nurtured a new hope for its future. The NHCC of today will not be the church
it was twenty, thirty, or forty years ago. Rather, it is leaning into a vocation
particularly suited for its present moment and current context. Pockets
of resistance remain at NHCC, and the long term future of this church
seems uncertain at best, but in the present moment the congregation's life
and witness appear stronger and healthier than it has been in years.

Members of the church will tell you that Kathleen's pastoral skills and
personal dynamism have reinvigorated a church that had been written
off by denominational executives. Some of the new life at NHCC can be
attributed to Kathleen's pastoral voice, a voice that was neither quick nor
easy to find. Kathleen desperately wants to experience the sense of having
arrived as a pastor, but so much about ministry seems open-ended and
context-specific to her. For this reason, she feels like she is always in the
process of arriving. She still overcommits and overextends, and she does
not enjoy life away from church and ministry as often or as much as she
would like, but over time she has found a way to express the heart of the
gospel through her ministry. Central to her learning has been the intentional times of reflection, often with colleagues and ministry coaches, that
have allowed her to process events, reappraise situations, and engage opportunities with increased wisdom and energy. As a result, Kathleen often
finds her stride in calling forth the gifts of others and then collaborating
with those individuals on specific ministries that convey God's hope and
healing and practice resurrection in concrete ways. It is a very good start
for someone who graduated from seminary only three years ago.

8

Beginning Strong, Finishing Well

I couldn't shut up about the food pantry.[1]

—SARA MILES

OPPORTUNITIES TO GROW IN VOICE

PEOPLE IN YOUR CONGREGATIONS may compliment you by saying, "You really have grown this year." Perhaps they have noticed that you exude more confidence and grace than when you began. Or maybe in performing certain pastoral roles, you have conveyed to them an increased appreciation for those particular aspects of ministry. Or possibly your recent comments and insights have revealed a broader, deeper grasp of what is at stake in congregational conversations. The members and friends in teaching congregations take great joy in offering this affirmation. Receive their words with thanksgiving for they are saying, "You are finding your voice."

I believe that people who offer you words of encouragement are also inviting you to continue to deepen your pastoral voice and practice. Pastors do not emerge from the womb, or from seminary, fully formed. We learn the practice of ministry by engaging in the practice of ministry. Those of you who take that learning seriously after seminary will sustain effective and imaginative ministry over the course of a pastoral career. That does not mean you will not make mistakes along the way. You will

1. Miles, *Take This Bread*, 175.

miss cues and clues and misread situations. And sometimes you will show little energy or interest for the push and pull, the ambiguity and open-endedness, of pastoral ministry and a congregational system. But vital pastors look for areas of growth in their understanding and practice of ministry for as long as they are involved in congregational leadership.

In particular, I want to highlight three opportunities you have for growing your pastoral voice. The first opportunity occurs at the conclusion of your field education experience, which is a paradoxical occasion. On the one hand, you have just fulfilled one of the requirements for your preparation for ministry. You should celebrate! On the other hand, if you have really invested yourself in this experience, you will have discovered the practical ministries you need to learn in order to serve well as a pastor. Hopefully, you also will have identified those areas of improvement related to who you are as a person. Early on we often do not know what we do not know. A key part of ongoing self-assessment and growth is finding ways to discover what we do not know. We do this so that we can explore and address our limitations and shortcomings for the sake of expressing a more vibrant ministry.

Many supervised ministry programs ask students to articulate their personal and professional goals from the outset. While this can be a valuable exercise before you complete your formal preparation for ministry, in truth you will do yourself an invaluable service by crafting a learning covenant in the first few years following your field education. Such a covenant will guide your growth as you begin life as a pastor. Revising your learning covenant every three to five years will help you to keep engaged and growing in your ministry.

Lawrence Golemon believes that good seminaries develop competent beginners in ministry. Your pastoral voice will start to emerge in seminary as a broad range of learning experiences comes together; but that early voice will not yet have been stretched, polished, or internalized. This is accomplished through the daily and weekly rhythms of actual pastoral practice. Golemon contends that new clergy do not leave seminary with a lack of relevant knowledge or skills, rather they simply do not yet have the necessary seasoning to harness the knowledge and skills that are so central to strong and imaginative pastoral leadership.[2] As writer Ray Bradbury says, after a while, the work takes on a certain rhythm and we

2. Golemon, "What Seminaries Do Well," 18.

notice the mechanical part of it less and less. Our guard goes down and the body takes over.[3]

The encouragement of Howard Thurman helps us to look to our growing edges. His words on the matter serve us well. "All around us," Thurman says, "old worlds are dying and new worlds are being born; all around us life is dying and new life is being born."[4] Much of what you will want and need to learn will present itself, in due time, through a wide range of the pastoral situations you experience. You will identify other things that particularly interest you or are especially pertinent to the ministry situation in which you find yourself. Keep looking to the growing edge in all of these moments and allow the natural seasoning that occurs through experience to enhance your pastoral voice.

A second opportunity for growth comes in your transition from seminary to church. You will have spent years preparing for this very transition. You will be excited and eager, but like any transition, it involves loss and uncertainty as well. Many graduates are not prepared for the grief that comes from leaving the support and friendship of their seminary community. Others are surprised by how much they depended on the rhythm of school to structure their days, and so they struggle terribly when they must decide how to allocate their time and where to set their own goals and deadlines.

Statistics about attrition during the first five years of ministry vary widely, but widespread agreement exists about one thing: Even for the best students and the most motivated ministers, the first five years after seminary represents a very challenging time. Some things in ministry will come easily to you. These are the things that resonate with you and match your gifts and personality well. You will have a seemingly endless amount of energy for them. When they are options, you will not be able to say "Yes" quickly enough. Other things will not come so easily for you, and they may even repulse you to think about them. For these efforts, the well of energy is shallow and dries up quickly. Before you say "No" to them, consider how they might contribute to your pastoral voice. Imagine settings in the future that you will be able to handle with more care and courage as a result of engaging those things now. And note, always, what you are learning about yourself as you engage in these areas of ministry.

---

3. Bradbury, *Zen in the Art of Writing*, 129.

4. Thurman, *Mood of Christmas*, 23.

The ministries of some very gifted people have been consistently under-mined because these individuals did not give sufficient attention to their wounds and vulnerabilities.

Carol Pinkham Oak argues that the pastoral experience that follows seminary is particularly significant because the habits and patterns for an entire ministry career are put in place during those first two years.[5] This truth puts a lot of pressure on your early years in ministry. Indeed, I recognize Oak's concern, and I affirm the importance of beginning a ministry well; and if you engage in the adaptation and learning that Oak espouses in her article, you will be able to reflect continuously upon your ministry and take steps toward ever-greater effectiveness. The path may be easier if you get most of this right from the start, but that does not mean you will not learn a lot along the way. You will. Identifying and unlearning bad habits and then developing healthier ones is part of the journey. As William Stafford writes:

> They want a wilderness with a map—
> but how about errors that give a new start?—[6]

Fortunately, people have recognized the difficulty of the early years of ministry and have created resources to help with the transition. The Lilly Endowment of Indianapolis has funded a number of initiatives such as peer groups, ministry residencies, mentoring strategies, and other transition into ministry programs. Generally, church judicatories are at-tuned to the challenges of this transition and can provide moral support, but such organizations usually are not able to lend financial assistance toward the process.

Most of the responsibility for finding your pastoral voice will fall to you. And what works for you may not work for someone else. One person reports that a peer group following seminary kept her in ministry long enough to understand what she was supposed to be doing. Another per-son did not find a peer group to be particularly helpful, but did find value in alternated weekly meetings between a therapist and a ministry coach. It may take you some effort to find what suits you best. But if fulfilling

---

5. Oak, "Creating Conditions for New Pastors' Success," 21.

6. Stafford, "A Course in Creative Writing," 195.

your call to ministry is important to you, then you will continue your search until you find what sustains your growth as a pastor.

A third opportunity for growth lies in that moment when you commit to flourishing in ministry.[7] I encourage you to make that commitment sooner rather than later. This is the time to think not just about how you want to begin your ministry, but also how you want to finish your ministry and what you need to put in place now in order to finish well at the end of your career. You cannot make up in the last two years of a ministry career for thirty years of bad habits and lackluster engagement.

If ministry stirs your soul and claims your energy, if ministry is really worth doing, if you have invested time and resources in preparing for ministry, if you are going to spend the next twenty or thirty or forty years performing this work, why not have the time of your life doing it? Mediocrity and casual indifference do not honor God. Many ministers find themselves relatively well established in their vocation and yet they are quite unhappy, tired, and disillusioned. Some remain in ministry only because they cannot find other work with comparable pay or work environment.

Other pastors, however, have sustained pastoral excellence over the seasons and continue to approach ministry with fresh energy and profound hope. They have encountered their share of loss, endured church and community conflicts, and navigated religious and cultural shifts that have waylaid many of their colleagues; but day after day, week in and week out, they engage ministry with focus, faith, and a startling openness to further growth. This does not mean that every day goes smoothly for them, nor does it mean that these ministers have a ready answer for every situation, or that all doubt and uncertainty have been erased for them. Rather, those who are flourishing in ministry recognize challenges, questions, and uncertainties as being opportunities to help them clarify their pastoral voice, nurture their imagination and agility, and lean more fully into the new world that God has proposed. If you engage ministry in this manner then, over time, you will become increasingly comfortable with who you are as a person and pastor, and how you deploy your gifts and passions. In this way, your pastoral voice will become a deep and enduring source of energy and hope.

---

7. See Matt Bloom's work, "Wellbeing at Work." The work includes research in the area of flourishing in ministry.

In *Take This Bread*, Sara Miles describes her fascinating spiritual journey, which for her included a Eucharistic experience that, in turn, led her to start opening food pantries throughout the city of San Francisco. In the process, Miles discovered that she could not shut up about the food pantry.[8] It was her passion. It was the avenue through which she understood and expressed her faith. As Miles demonstrates, a key part of flourishing in ministry is to find what you cannot shut up about. Stay close to what excites and animates you. Envision situations that would be blessed by what enlivens you. Develop approaches to put your values into practice. See these efforts as natural extensions of yourself and your ministry. This does not mean that you can stop doing everything else that falls to you as a pastor. Nor does it mean that everyone will share your particular excitement, but your enthusiasm may well cause others to discover what they themselves cannot keep quiet about. For you, making and acting on such a discovery will energize your ministry and sustain you through difficulty, distraction, and boredom.

Ray Bradbury, the great American author, described what passionate engagement in work means. Suffice it to say that the advice he gave to his fellow writers also applies to pastors: "If you are writing without zest, without gusto, without love, without fun, you are only half a writer. For the first thing a writer should be is—excited, . . . a thing of fevers and enthusiasms."[9]

Bradbury said that we eventually learn a new word for work.[10] I agree. If you give yourself to something, if you stay at it and with it, learn about it and learn from it, you will learn a new word for ministry. And that word is *love*.

So go ahead, consider what God desires for the world and give yourself to it. Give yourself to ministry. Find your voice.

Congregations and communities everywhere are listening.

8. Miles, *Take This Bread*, 266.

9. Bradbury, *Zen in the Art of Writing*, 4.

10. Ibid, 146.

Appendix A

Tools for Contextual Analysis

THIS APPENDIX CONTAINS IDEAS and questions you can use to go about observing, listening, gathering, and interpreting a particular context. In addition, this appendix is designed to help you develop your own questions so that you can study your particular context more deeply. . For other contextual analysis approaches and resources, see the relevant chapters in the following books: *Studying Congregations*, edited by Nancy Ammerman et al, and *From Our Doorsteps* by Rick Morse.

OBSERVING

Begin by walking through your church's neighborhood two or three times at various times during the day and on different days of the week. Take a map with you and record what you see, hear, and feel. You will want to make record of this area both in close-up detail and from a more panoramic viewpoint. If you are able to place yourself in the perspectives of others, then imagine walking through the neighborhood in another's shoes: first as a young family with small children, new to the community, then as a single person, then as an immigrant family, then as a single parent, then as an older couple. This may be difficult to do, so you may want to ask people who embody those perspectives to join you on your walks. These people will naturally see the world from their perspective. Ask yourself these questions:

- What do you see in this neighborhood?
- What do you hear in this neighborhood?
- What stands out to you, either for its beauty, neglect, or uniqueness?
- What other faith communities and houses of worship do you see?

- What other organizations or agencies are present in the area around the church?

- What goes on around the church through the week?

- Who else is here with you? How can you learn more about them? Is there something to learn from them?

- What is the appearance and condition of the church's grounds and buildings, and how does that compare with other properties in the area?

- If the congregation ceased to exist, how would the wider community be affected?

- What have you seen that you want to know more about?

LISTENING

Listen to the stories that members and friends of the congregation tell about the area where the church is located. You are attempting to answer the essential question, "What is life like here?"

Identify people, some from within the congregation and some from the wider community, who are willing to talk with you one-to-one as you conduct your contextual analysis. These people, ideally, will have varying degrees of familiarity with the area around the church. The interviews will help you develop a sympathetic, discerning understanding of what is at work beneath the surface of a given story. Through these interviews you will begin to learn not just about the actions and events of these stories, but what values and priorities motivated and influenced those actions and events.

In regard to identifying the people from within the congregation to interview (a minimum of two), select individuals who are capable of describing what life is like in the area around the church, not within the church itself. Plan to meet with each of these people at least two to three times. Ideally, your interviewees will include someone who has a long history in the area and someone who is relatively new to the area. The former will be aware of changes over time, and you should ask about those changes. Conversely, encourage the newcomer to talk about aspects of the community that are interesting, unusual, or appalling—the things that brought this person into the community or would have given them second thoughts.

In both cases, the first conversation may indeed bring out important items for discussion and exploration. However, it is more likely that the first conversation will be slow going. You might have to prod people to look at something that they have not considered being all that important in the past. Subsequent interviews likely will be much more helpful to your study: people will have had time to reflect on their first conversation with you and, more often than not, their interest in your study will sharpen their own observational skills. Just as critically, you will probably find that most people will want to talk about life within the congregation. Do what you can to prevent these conversations from turning inward. Remind your interviewees that, at that moment, you are interested in learning about life around the church, not within it. You can tell interviewees that you will be asking them about the church's story, key players, and major turning points later on.

Regarding interviews with people who are not members of the congregation, your most likely candidates will be church neighbors who are visible in the area or people who work in nearby businesses, schools, or community agencies. In addition to hearing their perspectives on whether the area is flourishing, maintaining, or declining, you might also ask what they know about the church where you serve.

The following questions will aid in your discovery:

- How has the area around the church changed in the time you have been attending this church?
- What is this area best known for in the wider community?
- What are the conflicts at play in the area around the church?
- Where are the formal and informal gathering places?
- Who lives, works, and plays in this area of town?
- What are the cycles and seasons of this place?
- What are the most important institutions in this area?
- How well is the church known in this area?
- Is the area rich with or lacking in diversity, and what kinds of diversity are represented?
- Who are the invisible people in this area and why?[1]

---

1 Ammerman et al., *Studying Congregations*, 42.

- What invisible forces are at play here, either for good or ill?

- How is the church involved in the area (the immediate context)? Is it involved?

GATHERING

After you have observed and listened, you are ready to begin gathering historical, cultural, and demographic information. It is worth noting that, in the past, the gathering of information, especially demographic information (population, educational levels, per capita income averages), was often the starting point for congregational visioning processes. The upshot, however, was that leadership teams rarely knew what to do with these data once it was gathered. That is, leadership did not understand how the demographic data connected to the living world around them. By contrast, as you compile demographics and collect other information, the observation and listening you have done already will give you ideas about what life is like in the area surrounding the church, and enables you to look for connections. Know this: A dominant group that reviews only demographic information typically confirms its own biases, which in turn can cause this group to dismiss emerging trends and opportunities as being statistically insignificant.

The following are helpful resources for performing a demographic analysis:

- www.zipwho.com

- www.zipskinny.com

- www.esri.com/data/esri_data/tapestry.html

- www.photovault.com provides a wonderful visual that highlights the significance of context (at www.photovault.com/Link/Cities/Cities-Master.html, pictures rotate from all of the U.S. states and from many places around the world)

- www.link2lead.com or www.perceptgroup.com/Percept-Home.aspx

- the Hartford Institute for Religious Research's study of Faith Communities Today (FACT) at www.hartfordinstitute.org/cong/nondenom_FACT.html

While gathering information from these resources, you will want to explore questions such as:

- In what ways have the demographics changed over the last ten years? Twenty years?

- What groups of people do the numbers call attention to that you have not noticed to this point?

- What is the content and nature of the religious landscape around the church?

- What predictions have been made about future growth patterns? Are there accompanying plans in place for roads, infrastructure, schools, parks, and other public institutions?

- Where do church members live in relation to the church? What are their typical traffic patterns and where are the areas they do not go?

- What has been written about the area that will give you an idea of what life is like here?

- How has the area been captured in art or music or literature?

- What newspaper articles reveal major issues, shifts, or conflicts for the area?

In addition to understanding the immediate context for the congregation's life and work, broader cultural trends have their own implications for ministry. For example, what is the impact of having as many as five different generations, each with its own worldview and set of priorities, active in a single congregation? Or how does the common mantra of being "spiritual but not religious" play out in your church? Or what have been the effects of raging debates over social issues?

The following extensive surveys and information can help you engage in a discussion about broader cultural trends:

- The Pew Forum on Religion and Public Life (www.pewforum.org)

- The Association of Religion Data Archives (www.thearda.com)

- The American Religious Identification Survey, or ARIS (www.americanreligionsurvey-aris.org)

- ReligiousTolerance.org (www.religioustolerance.org)

- George Barna's research (www.barna.org)

From these resources you can gain an appreciation for the changing landscape on which your church finds itself. Not every congregation will engage every one of these issues, but many of these issues will at least be recognizable to them. Numerous congregations will have struggled already—or are struggling presently—with them and their impacts.

INTERPRETING

After observing, listening, and gathering information, you will be in a position to form some initial interpretations about the place where you have been called to do ministry. Stand back for a moment and look for emerging patterns and the areas that require further questioning. Interpretative work also allows you and the people in your congregation to be honest about the reality around the church, which is no small feat. The following questions are designed to help you carry out your interpretative work:

- What can you say about this place from your observing, listening, and gathering information?

- What questions about this place have emerged from your observing activities?

- Are the data you gleaned from your listening and gathering activities consistent; and are your findings consistent enough to allow you to form a fairly reliable picture of this place?

- What consistent patterns and themes have emerged from your research?

- What inconsistencies and contradictions do you need to explore further?

- What do you need to do in order to suspend judgment long enough so that you can explore these seeming contradictions?

- Where do you perceive God in this context; and what themes from the Christian story intersect with the issues that are at play in the context?

- In what ways does the context appear to shape and influence the congregation, and vice-versa?

- To what extent does the context appear to impact congregational mood, confidence, and direction?

- What contextual issues call for investigation, reflection, and action?

Appendix B

Tools for Congregational Study

THIS APPENDIX PROVIDES YOU with questions that allow you to conduct a congregational study. You are engaging the study in order to answer the essential question, "What is life like in this congregation and what people, traditions, and experiences have shaped that life?"

The approach for this investigation includes the same four steps as does the contextual analysis—observing, listening, gathering, and interpreting. It is a process that is designed to help you gain a thorough familiarity with a congregation's life and witness. Note that the following questions are organized in a somewhat arbitrary manner: Many of them could be listed as resources for each of the four categories. Nonetheless, the organization provides a solid foundation from which you can build your own study.

Other helpful resources for this investigation include the following books: *Studying Congregations* by Nancy Ammerman et al, *The Hidden Lives of Congregations* by Israel Galindo, and *From Our Doorsteps* by Rick Morse.

OBSERVING

Walk through your church. Walk the church grounds and neighborhood. Visit at various times during the day, and on different days of the week. Consider the following questions and record what you discover:

- What do you see and hear when the congregation gathers for worship, study, fellowship, and mission?
- Can you identify what is sacred to the congregation?
- What is a key symbol for the congregation?

- Are there clues to the congregation's theology?

- What appears to be the spirit of the congregation—bold, tentative, passive, pessimistic, depressed, gentle, confident, anxious, etc.?

- Are there noticeable conflicts?

- Where do you perceive the power center of the congregation to be?

- Who are the key actors in the congregation and what regular participants seem to play lesser roles?

- Can you describe the dynamics and conflicts that are at play at your ministry site (life cycle, size, spirituality, and identity); and can you determine whether these conflicts appear to be energizing or polarizing the congregation?

- When you consider the interior of the church building(s), what is conveyed by its appearance, traffic flow, room arrangement, signage, and style?

- Based on how you see the congregation spending its time, money, and energy, what would you say is the mission of the congregation?

- What are some ways that the church positively impacts the immediate area around it?

- Based on what you have observed, how would you define the congregation's mission?

- What stories about the congregation seem to be particularly important to its participants and to the congregation as a whole?

- If the congregation ceased to exist, in what church, if any, do you think its participants would become involved?

- What similarities do you see between the people in the area around the church who do not participate in the congregation and the people who are participants in the congregation?

LISTENING

Identify at least two people who are active in the congregation who can speak honestly about the congregation, and who bring different perspectives on the congregation, and then ask them to describe the congregation's life and witness. The following questions are designed to help you focus this investigation.

- How has the congregation changed over the years in terms of organization, spirit, membership, programs, leadership, and level of participation?
- How has the congregation reacted or responded to change in the community over the years—by ignoring, resisting, relocating, sharpening identity, innovating, or adopting a whole new identity?
- Who have been the most influential people in the church's history?
- Are the stated leaders and the actual leaders the same people?
- What have been the losses in the church and community and how have they been named and dealt with?
- What are the five most important events, programs, and ministries in the congregation?
- What will the congregation be like in twenty years?
- If you could tell only one story about your church, what would it be and why would you choose that story?
- What other institutions, groups, and organizations in your area vie for people's time, energy, money, and loyalty?
- How does the congregation think of itself and what does the congregation consider to be its calling?
- What stories about the congregation seem to be particularly important to the congregation?

GATHERING

The following questions are designed to help you to gather important information about a congregation:

- What do the numbers for membership, worship attendance, giving, and spending over the last forty years, reported at five-year intervals, suggest about the congregation's story? (Numbers don't tell everything about a church, but they can sometimes provide important clues about the life and witness of a congregation.)

- What do congregational histories, newsletters, and other internal publications reveal about the congregation?

- What do newspaper articles, pictures, and books about the church suggest about the congregation's story?

- Apart from the formal story of the congregation's history, what twists and turns have brought the congregation to where it is today? (Note that truly important events may only be hinted at in a formal historical account.)

INTERPRETING

After observing, listening, and gathering information, you will be in a position to form some initial interpretations about the life and witness of a congregation. The following questions are designed to help you carry out your interpretative work:

- From what you have observed, heard, and gathered, create a congregational timeline. When was the congregation most alive, what did that look like then, and what contributed to that vitality within the congregation and beyond it?

- What issues are raised by your denominational relationship or nondenominational status?

- What do you perceive about the level of trust, conflict, and the way decisions are made?

- What patterns and themes have emerged?

- What contradictions need further exploration?

- From the minimal introduction you have received to the congregation, what impact do you think the congregation has on its immediate context?

- What gifts of leadership and talent are present in the congregation?

- What opportunities for ministry are present in the congregation and the immediate context; and to what extent is the congregation engaging its immediate context?

Bibliography

Allen, Ronald J. *A Faith of Your Own: Naming What You Really Believe.* Louisville: Westminster John Knox, 2010.

Ammerman, Nancy, Jackson W. Carroll, Carl S. Dudley, and William McKinney, eds. *Studying Congregations: A New Handbook.* Nashville: Abingdon, 1998.

Bailie, Gil. *Violence Unveiled: Humanity at the Crossroads.* New York: Crossroad, 1996.

Bass, Diana Butler. "Living the Story." *Alban e-Weekly,* January 22, 2007.

Berry, Wendell. *Imagination in Place.* Berkeley, CA: Counterpoint, 2010.

———. *Standing by Words.* Washington, D.C.: Shoemaker and Hoard, 2005.

Bloom, Matt. "Wellbeing at Work." Online at www.wellbeing.nd.edu/The-Research-Team. html.

Bodenhamer, David J., and Robert G. Barrows, eds. *The Encyclopedia of Indianapolis.* Bloomington, IN: IU Press, 1994.

Bradbury, Ray. *Zen in the Art of Writing: Releasing the Creative Genius Within You.* New York: Bantam, 1990.

Brueggemann, Walter. *Journey to the Common Good.* Louisville, KY: Westminster John Knox, 2010.

Buechner, Frederick. *Telling Secrets.* New York: HarperOne, 1992.

Cahalan, Kathleen. "Introducing Ministry and Fostering Integration: Teaching the Bookends of the Master of Divinity Program." In *For Life Abundant: Practical Theology, Theological Education and Christian Ministry,* 91–115. Eds. Dorothy C. Bass and Craig Dykstra. Grand Rapids, MI: William B. Eerdmans, 2008.

Callahan, Kennon L. *Small, Strong Congregations.* San Francisco: Jossey-Bass, 2000.

Childress, Kyle. "Good Work: Learning Ministry from Wendell Berry," *Christian Century,* March 8, 2005, 28–33.

Covey, Stephen R. *The Seven Habits of Highly Effective People.* New York: Simon and Schuster, 1989.

Dunn, Stephen. *Walking Light.* New York: W. W. Norton, 1993.

Dykstra, Craig. "Pastoral and Ecclesial Imagination." In *For Life Abundant: Practical Theology, Theological Education and Christian Ministry,* 41–61. Eds. Dorothy C. Bass and Craig Dykstra. Grand Rapids, MI: William B. Eerdmans, 2008.

Faulkner, William. "Banquet Speech" (Nobel Banquet lecture at the City Hall, Stockholm, Sweden, December 10, 1950).

Fluker, Walter Earl, and Catherine Tumber. *A Strange Freedom: The Best of Howard Thurman on Religious Experience and Public Life.* Boston: Beacon, 1998.

Frank, Thomas Edward. *The Soul of the Congregation: An Invitation to Congregational Reflection.* Nashville: Abingdon, 2000.

Bibliography

Friedman, Edwin H. *The Failure of Nerve: Leadership in the Age of the Quick Fix.* New York: Seabury, 2007.

———. *Generation to Generation: Family Process in Church and Synagogue.* New York: Guilford, 1985.

Galindo, Israel. *The Hidden Lives of Congregations: Discerning Church Dynamics.* Herndon, VA: The Alban Institute, 2004.

Golemon, Lawrence. "What Seminaries Do Well," *Congregations,* no. 4 (2006), 17–19.

Graham, Elaine. *Transforming Practice: Pastoral Theology in an Age of Uncertainty.* New York: Mowbray, 1996.

Hamm, Richard L. *Recreating the Church: Leadership for the Postmodern Age.* St. Louis, MO: Chalice, 2007.

Hanh, Thich Nhat. *Touching Peace: Practicing the Art of Mindful Living.* Berkeley, CA: Parallax, 1992.

Harrison, Beverly Wildung. "Keeping Faith in a Sexist Church." In *Making the Connections: Essays in Feminist Social Ethics,* 206–34. Ed. Carol S. Robb. Boston: Beacon, 1985.

Hart, Mark. "Focusing Upon Skill Development." In *Courageous Conversations: The Teaching and Learning of Pastoral Supervision,* 1–12. Ed., William R. DeLong. Lanham, MD: University Press of America, 2010.

Heifetz, Ronald, Alexander Grashow, and Marty Linsky. *The Practice of Adaptive Leadership: Tools and Tactics for Changing Your Organization and the World.* Boston: Harvard Business Press, 2009.

Herring, Laraine. *Writing Begins with the Breath: Embodying Your Authentic Voice.* Boston: Shambhala, 2007.

Hester, Richard L., and Kelli Walker-Jones. *Know Your Story and Lead with It: The Power of Narrative in Clergy Leadership.* Herndon, VA: The Alban Institute, 2009.

Hotchkiss, Dan. *Governance and Ministry: Rethinking Board Leadership.* Herndon, VA: The Alban Institute, 2009.

Hough, Joseph C., and John B. Cobb Jr. *Christian Identity and Theological Education.* Atlanta: Scholars Press, 1985.

Hunter, Victor. *Desert Hearts and Healing Fountains: Gaining Pastoral Vocational Clarity.* St. Louis, MO: Chalice, 2003.

Kingsolver, Barbara. *Animal Dreams.* New York: HarperCollins, 1990.

Lamott, Anne. *Bird by Bird: Some Instructions on Writing and Life.* New York: Anchor, 1994.

Leas, Speed B. *Discover Your Conflict Management Style.* Herndon, VA: The Alban Institute, 1997.

Loomer, Bernard. "S-I-Z-E Is the Measure." In *Religious Experience and Process Theology: The Pastoral Implications of a Major Modern Movement,* 69–76. Eds. Cargas, Harry James, and Bernard Lee. New York: Paulist, 1976.

Lyon, K. Brynolf, and Dan P. Moseley. *How to Lead in Church Conflict: Healing Ungrieved Loss.* Nashville: Abingdon, 2012.

MacDonald, George. "God's Calling Plan." *Leadership* 24 (2003), 35–42.

Maxwell, Florida Scott. *The Measure of My Days.* New York: Penguin, 1983.

Miles, Sara. *Take This Bread.* New York: Ballantine, 2007.

Montaldo, Jonathan, ed. *A Year with Thomas Merton: Daily Meditations from His Journals.* San Francisco: HarperCollins, 2004.

Mooty, Robert. Ordination Sermon (preached May 20, 2001, Timberlake Christian Church, Lynchburg, Virginia).

Morse, Rick. *From Our Doorsteps*. St. Louis, MO: Chalice, 2010.

Moseley, Dan. "Playing Jazz: Leading in Liquid Times" (presented at the Hal Watkins Lecture on Leadership, National City Christian Church, Washington, D.C., April 21, 2006).

Norris, Kathleen. *Dakota: A Spiritual Geography*. Boston: Houghton-Mifflin, 1993.

Oak, Carol Pinkham. "Creating Conditions for New Pastors' Success," *Congregations*, no. 4 (2006), 20–25.

Obama, Barack. *Dreams from My Father: A Story of Race and Inheritance*. New York: Three Rivers, 2004.

Oswald, Roy M., and Otto Kroeger. *Pesonality Type and Religious Leadership*. Herndon, VA: The Alban Institute, 1988.

Palmer, Parker. *Let Your Life Speak: Listening for the Voice of Vocation*. San Francisco: Jossey-Bass, 2000.

Proctor, Samuel DeWitt, and Gardner C. Taylor. *We Have This Ministry: The Heart of the Pastor's Vocation*. Valley Forge, PA: Judson, 1996.

Rohr, Richard. *Contemplation in Action*. New York: Crossroad, 2006.

Shaughnessy, Susan. *Walking on Alligators: A Book of Meditation for Writers*. New York: HarperCollins, 1993.

Sittler, Joseph. *The Ecology of Faith*. Philadelphia: Muhlenberg, 1959.

Smith, Luther E., Jr. *Howard Thurman: Essential Writings*. Maryknoll, NY: Orbis, 2006.

Sprinkle, Stephen V. *Ordination: Celebrating the Gift of Ministry*. St. Louis, MO: Chalice, 2004.

Stafford, William. "A Course in Creative Writing." *The Way It Is: New and Selected Poems*. Saint Paul, MN: Graywolf, 1999.

———. "Ask Me." *The Way It Is: New and Selected Poems*. Saint Paul, MN: Graywolf, 1999.

Steinke, Peter L. *Congregational Leadership in Anxious Times: Being Calm and Courageous No Matter What*. Herndon, VA: The Alban Institute, 2006.

———. *How Your Church Family Works: Understanding Congregations as Emotional Systems*. Herndon, VA: The Alban Institute, 1993.

Thurman, Howard. *The Mood of Christmas*. Richmond, IN: Friends United Press, 1973.

———. "The Sound of the Genuine" (baccalaureate address at Spelman College, May 4, 1980).

Turner, Mary Donovan, and Mary Lin Hudson. *Saved from Silence: Finding Women's Voice in Preaching*. St. Louis, MO: Chalice, 1999.

Vecchione, Patrice. *Writing and the Spiritual Life: Finding Your Voice by Looking Within*. New York: McGraw-Hill, 2001.

Warford, Malcolm L. *Becoming a New Church*. Cleveland, OH: United Church Press, 2000.

West, Don. Eds. Jeff Biggers and George Brosi. *No Lonesome Road: Selected Prose and Poems*. Urbana, IL: University of Illinois Press, 2004.

Willimon, William H. *Pastor: The Theology and Practice of Ordained Ministry*. Nashville: Abingdon, 2002.